DEVELOPING INSTITUTION: A GUIDE FOR SUB-SAHARA AFRICA

DEVELOPING INSTITUTION: A GUIDE FOR SUB-SAHARA AFRICA

Organizational Management

Dr. Q. Somah Paygai, Sr.

Copyright © 2015 by Dr. Q. Somah Paygai, Sr.

ISBN:	Softcover	978-1-5035-6244-8
	eBook	978-1-5035-6243-1

All rights reserved. No part of this book may be reproduced or transmitted in any form or by any means, electronic or mechanical, including photocopying, recording, or by any information storage and retrieval system, without permission in writing from the copyright owner.

Any people depicted in stock imagery provided by Thinkstock are models, and such images are being used for illustrative purposes only.
Certain stock imagery © Thinkstock.

Print information available on the last page.

Rev. date: 05/14/2015

To order additional copies of this book, contact:
Xlibris
1-888-795-4274
www.Xlibris.com
Orders@Xlibris.com
711030

CONTENTS

Abstract vii
Acknowledgements ix
Abbreviations Used xi
Introduction/Background 1
    Purpose 2
    Definition 2
    Economic Community of West African States 3
    Main Findings 3
    The current financial crisis 3
    Ministries of education and universities 4
    Management development 5
    Experience of the Agencies 5
    Implications for Policy 7
    Specific Recommendations 9
    Support for adequacy of financing for administrative
        services 9
    Focus on institutional development 9
    Development of efficient organization and methods 10
    Expanded staff training 10
    Provision of buildings and equipment 11
    The provision of information resources 11
    Strengthening Management Development 11
    Support for the Management of Vocational Training 12
    Strengthening Universities 13
Problems And Needs Of Institution Building In
    Management Development And Training 15
    Management Development 16
The European Experience 18
    Coordination 41
    Financing and Autonomy 42

> Staffing 43
> Limitations in Mandates and Scope 44
> Problem of Response to Labor Market Requirements 49
> The Financing of Training 52
> Managerial Personnel 54
> Conclusion 56

Experience In Institutional Development 57
> The Experience of ILO 57
> Management development 57
> Management of vocational training 60
> The Experience of UNESCO 65
> Bank Experience in Education Lending 68

Bibliography 75
Index 79

Abstract

This study is an effort to improve management operations in the Economic Community of West African States (ECOWAS). It is prompted by the appearance of a crisis in management development brought on by the difficult financial situation in which most countries, particularly Liberia, Sierra Leone, and Guinea, found themselves by the 1990s. Growth and change in the management systems of Sub-Sahara Africa (Liberia, Sierra Leone, and Guinea) had been achieved during the 1970s and 1980s, but serious problems had arisen in the 1990s regarding how to sustain these expanded systems of management and training. In part, the problems were financial; in part, they were institutional, but in the final analysis, the failure lay in resource management and planning.

The Economic Community of West African States (ECOWAS) ought to understand that what is needed is not yet another set of external recommendations to the countries on how to chart their development. Rather, there is a need for an understanding of why these countries, after decades of bank lending and other external aid, still appeared to be in need of external participation in the analysis of their problems.

Acknowledgements

Many people have assisted in the preparation of this "BOOK". To my late mother, Mrs. Tetee Vambran-Paygai who instilled the virtue of education in me. My siblings, Reuben, Arthur, Julia, and brother-in-law Moses Bee. They opened their homes and hearts to my family during my absence from the United States of America.

The person most responsible for this project is my wife, Lucia. She endured many difficult years of my schooling and in almost every endeavour in my life. Lucia encouraged me throughout this project and I sincerely dedicate this book to my wife, Lucia Boakai Toweh-Paygai and our sons, Douglas, Charles, and Q. Somah (STONE) Paygai, Jr. This book has taken me on a journey I did not expect. I'm glad that it took this long, but the book turned out as anticipated.

Thanks!

Abbreviations Used

CEAO—Communaute Economique de l'Afrique de l'Quest (West African Economic Community)
CESAG—Centre Africain d'Etudes Superieures en Gestion (African Center for Higher Management Studies)
CIADFOR—Centre interafricain pour le developpement de la formation professionnelle (Inter-African Center for the Development of Vocational Training)
IIEP—International Institute for Educational Planning
ILO—International Labour Organization
IMF—International Monetary Fund
NPC—National Productivity Center
O and M—organization and methods
UK—United Kingdom
UNDP—United Nations Development Programme
UNESCO—United Nations Educational Scientific and Cultural Organization
(Other abbreviations are explained in the text wherever they occur.)

Introduction/Background

(a) Background

1. This study forms part of an effort to intensify and improve operations in Sub-Sahara Africa. It was prompted by the appearance of a crisis in management development brought on by the extraordinarily difficult financial situation in which most countries found themselves by the 1990s. Not all the economic measures being considered or taken in the sector appeared to be in the best long-term interest of the countries. Growth and change in the systems of Sub-Sahara Africa had been achieved during the 1960s, 1970s, and 1980s, but serious problems had arisen in the 1990s and 2000s regarding how to sustain these expanded systems of management and training. In part, the problems were financial; in part, they were institutional, but in the final analysis, the failure lay in resource management and planning. Hence, it seemed that what was needed was not yet another set of external recommendations to the countries on how to chart their development, but rather (a) an understanding of why these countries, after decades of Bank lending and other external aid, still appeared to be in need of considerable external participation in the analysis of their problems in the planning and implementation of development in the sector, and in the efficient management of education and training; and (b) some idea of the steps to be taken to build up strong permanent national capacity in these areas.

2. For this study, institutional development was taken to mean the establishment, strengthening, or enhancement of the capacity of agencies or institutions to perform their assigned functions efficiently. This means providing a system that includes an unequivocal mandate, goals, and objectives, the necessary physical facilities (buildings, equipment, and furniture), personnel of sufficient caliber and the required numbers, a rational organization, well thought-out procedures, and the necessary authority and financial resources. It also means facilitating the authority and financial resources; it also means facilitating the continuous evaluation, maintenance, and updating of this overall system.
3. The study reviews selected aspects of institutional development in management and training. It examines the administration of ministries of education, educational planning, and educational research. Universities were included because of their vital role in preparing high-level man power in certain disciplines considered crucial in management, planning, and research in the education and training system but also because it plays, or ought to play, a direct role in the preparation and performance of managerial staff in organizations and training and other sectors.

a. Purpose

It was over a decade ago that the government of some African nations got together to draft a momentous document that they hoped would change the face of Africa, south of the Sahara. Their goal is perhaps the most important aspect of creating a common market that will encourage competition among member nations and keep the bureaucrats from unfairly exploiting the citizens' strengths. However, with the continuing changes in the world economy, there has been no concrete major document to transcend these goals into reality.

b. Definition

This book is geared toward creating the incentive whereby nations within this African region, south of the Sahara, will study carefully with the view of the pivotal issues confronting Africa, such as economic and monetary policy, economic integration, the custom union and free movement of goods, free movement of workers, special trading arrangements, development policy, regional policy, common commercial policy, and progress toward political union. All these aspects are totally missing, and they are referred to as institutional development.

c. Economic Community of West African States

The Economic Community of West African States was formed by sixteen leaders of some West African countries (Liberia, Togo, Mali, Ghana, Sierra Leone, Niger, Benin, Guinea, Burkina Faso, Nigeria, Senegal, Gambia, Ivory Coast, Gabon, Cameroun, and Guinea-Bissau).

The community founders fully realized that the creation of such organization and the effective implementation of common policies would have to be accompanied by a common economic policy. It was clear that the establishment of this community would lead to growing economic interdependence between the member states, making it more difficult for them to pursue their own short-term economic policy objectives. Conversely, economic measures adopted by one country would have a considerably greater impact on its partners as economic interdependence grew.

However, in April 22, 1978, the Economic Community of West African States (ECOWAS) adopted a protocol on nonaggression. Because of the community's inability to depoliticize and with no given mandate, it became a party to Liberia's civil strife. This action has caused the community to be on unstable grounds with West African Francophone countries. Presently, ECOWAS serves as a political organization with total disregard for its intended purpose of formation. There are no policies in place for implementation on the basis of economic interdependence.

(b) Main Findings

1. *The current financial crisis.* In recent years, there has been a financial crisis in the sector. The most important impact of this

has been to accelerate a decline in institutional capacity and infrastructure, which began some twenty years or so ago.
This decline needs to be addressed urgently and effectively.
2. In the three selected countries, an already-inadequate administrative service is being required to bear a disproportionate share of the cost-reduction efforts. Cost reduction efforts in the sector are falling most acutely on administrative overheads and research and on specific items—such as transport and supplies—that vitiate the productivity and effectiveness of administrative staff, ironically, even reducing their capacity to curb waste. These efforts are also having an impact on universities in ways that will restrict institutional development in management and training.
3. *Ministries of education and universities.* Even without specific reference to the financial crisis, the ministries of education in these countries encounter various fundamental problems. First of all, the status and reputation of educational management are relatively low. External aid agencies (and even governments themselves) fail to give due recognition to the scope and importance of the planning function and to the place of research in development. Secondly, the ministries lack qualified specialists in key areas, such as financial management and planning, educational planning, design and implementation of educational development (projects), statistics, educational research, public administration, business management, and educational administration. Thirdly, the available physical infrastructure for the functions of managing the system is substandard in both central and provincial offices, and essential equipment—such as data processing and office equipment and vehicles—is in short supply or nonexistent.

Fourthly, for reasons that are perfectly valid, the ministries have embarked on geographical decentralization of services; however, they have not been able to provide the necessary staff development programs to assure adequate services in the provinces.

In two cases, separate ministries have been created in recent years to attend exclusively to higher education—a measure that entails excessively high administrative overheads. Finally, the information resources needed for efficient management and planning are seriously deficient. The paucity of statistical data and library and documentation services in ministries, universities, and in the countries generally offers little basis for well-informed decision making.

4. *Management development.* In the field of management development and training, overall institutional weaknesses in Sub-Sahara African countries pose special problems. Large corporations look after their own interests, but the smaller, private-sector firms tend not to perceive their interests in organized programs for these purposes. There is urgent need for efficient umbrella institutional arrangements to coordinate initiatives; to promote employer participation in funding (instead of leaving funding entirely to the government); to promote the role of employers in the design and evaluation of training programs; to establish a range of training that has the flexibility to respond to their needs; to ensure the development of adequate information, research, and consulting services; and to develop and retain the right kind of managerial personnel required for training institutions. Management development suffers from mandates that are too restricted to (a) training alone, as distinct from a package of measures to strengthen management; (b) programs that can be funded immediately, as distinct from what is urgently needed, and (c) a very limited range of fields and strategies that neglects, among other things, the social sectors (including education), accounting and financial management, the management of development processes, in-plant training, and consulting.

Experience of the Agencies

This study looks at the experience of ILO, UNESCO, and the bank in institutional development in management and training in Sub-Sahara Africa (Guinea, Liberia, and Sierra Leone).

In regard to management development, the strategy that has grown out of the extensive experience of the ILO is (i) to strengthen the institutional framework in regard to policies, planning, research, and rationalization of training networks; (ii) to improve performance and increase the impact of management-development institutions and programs supporting these with preparing essential materials;

(iii) to address the neglected sectors; and (iv) to encourage regional, subregional, and interregional cooperation among management development institutions.

UNESCO has had long-standing experience in institutional development in the sector, not only through its International Institute for Education Planning but also through its field programs. On the basis of this experience, UNESCO stresses (i) the importance of government commitment to providing effective counterpart arrangements, (ii) government financial capacity to sustain the effort after withdrawal of UNESCO, (iii) the proper adaptation of institutional development, and (v) the need for an adequate local staffing arrangement to service external aid. UNESCO has seen its strategy develop toward providing expertise in more specific rather than general skills and through short-term rather than long-term assignment of experts. Also, it has seen its strategy development toward support for regional efforts such as the Network for Educational Innovation and Development in Africa (NEIDA), networking, technical cooperation among developing countries, and twinning in its search for effective ways of promoting institutional development in a variety of circumstances.

The World Bank has invested increasingly in institutional development in the sector all education projects since FY71, including such components. The principal areas to which institutional development financing has been directed have been (1) project management and educational planning (both areas of interest to the lending program and pipeline)—47 percent of items; (2) general management, with a view to strengthening central and provincial administration, management training, and the management of vocational training (28 percent of items); and (3) technical aspects of educational management, with a view to supporting qualitative changes and improvement in education (26 percent). The means adopted for effecting institutional development involved usually a mix of devices; however, it was predominantly that of expert services (in eighty-five of eighty-seven relevant projects), equipment and furniture in fifty-eight projects, fellowships in forty-eight projects, buildings in furniture in fifty-eight projects, fellowships in forty-eight projects, buildings in forty-six cases, and support for operating costs in thirty-four projects.

The major deficiencies in the design of these projects, from the institutional development standpoint, were (a) the relatively meager effort on behalf of central administrative capacity as a whole; (b) the general underutilization of fellowships and overreliance on expert services; and (c) the neglect of development of universities, especially in the strategic disciplines and the economic and social sciences—development that would have improved university capacity to provide a better quality of graduates and enhanced their consulting capacity.

Some fifty-eight of the one hundred projects approved for Sub-Sahara Africa FY64–84 were completed by March 1985. The review of the relevant project completion and audit reports reveals that the institutional development components were an often neglected area, not only in project implementation but also in project evaluation. These reports do show, however, that progress in institutionalizing project management capacity and in developing satisfactory educational planning capacity has been very limited, which appears to be the result of insufficient emphasis on training. Several of the large numbers of studies included in the projects were not done or were changed substantially for lack of local commitment to them. Assistance to the technical aspects of management of education has yielded several positive results, although the outcomes have been mixed. Efforts to strengthen management, including support for central and district administration and for management-training components, have been generally successful. The items concerning management of vocational training encountered some initial difficulties regarding employer support, but in general, outcomes have been good. Implementation experience with experts as a means of effecting institutional development has been largely negative. Often the experts were either not used or were not as effective as intended, ill times, unsupported by counterparts, or unmindful of training responsibilities (UNESCO, 1984).

Implications for Policy

It is essential to understand the meaning and nature of institutional development. It is the product of several separate ingredients working in harmony to develop and maintain institutional capacity—personnel of the right quality, motivation, skills and attitudes (including good leadership) and in sufficient number, efficient organization and procedures, adequate physical plant and financial resources, possession of a mandate and real authority to perform, access to the minimum financial resources needed for good performance, access to information that is as up-to-date as possible in the broad area of operation, and the ability to evaluate performance and modernize or adjust the overall institutional environment in the light of changing needs. Denial of access to any of these essentials at any given time can thwart institutional development efforts and can even rapidly erode capacities developed over a lengthy period.

The second important consideration is that each institution operates in its own social and cultural setting. The institutional needs at any given time will vary according to the mix of deficiencies and superfluities, given the objectives of the institution. Remedies and institutional development efforts, therefore, have to be tailor-made. One characteristic of the institutional environment is the interdependence of institutions. Excessive weakness in one militates against the achievement of efficiency in another institution, sometimes rendering it necessary to resolve the problem by reaching into the university or the ministry of planning, for example. The same holds good for sections of a ministry, where the weak can eventually neutralize the strong. The fundamental institutional problem in Sub-Sahara Africa is that too many of the requirements for institutional capacity are lacking, and too many of the institutions are weak, generally requiring a total bootstrap operation over a long period. The failures of earlier institution-building efforts have arisen because of the limited range of the efforts over aspects of the institutions over time and over the number of related institutions to which attention was devoted. Under colonialism, by deliberate metropolitan policy, there was widespread denial of access to knowledge, technology, manufacturing and general decision making. Thus, the challenge posed by independence was fundamentally and institutional one. Movement toward African institutional strength, therefore, threatens those whose perception of their interests developed around these institutional weaknesses and incapacities. These may include corporations whose structure and policy have evolved on an assumption that the institutional weaknesses in Africa will be perpetual, and they may include the individual expert who is reluctant to transfer his skills to the local counterpart and so render himself redundant.

Specific Recommendations

The following recommendations are put forward to address the particular problems and needs encountered. These fall well within the financial scope of existing operations and programs of assistance to the sector and merely require a change in focus and priorities.

1. *Support for adequacy of financing for administrative services.* Two of the most urgent needs in management systems are (a) greater real financial autonomy for ministries to determine the allocation of the financial resources made available for the sector and (b) the achievement of a realistic balance between the sector resources spent in the schools and the resources allocated to managing the institutional system.

   There is need for the analysis of expenditure on management with a view to discovering the amounts and proportions of sector funding spent on administration, the effectiveness of this expenditure, and its adequacy. Budget preparation and presentation need to be done in such a way as to highlight these financial ratios. Educational planning units need to address this issue in a more detailed manner and to map out a long-term strategy for correcting and imbalances.

2. *Focus on institutional development.* First of all, there is need for a stronger and more consistent focus on strengthening capacities to manage, plan, and research the sector. This means a greater number of institutional development components of development projects and a greater institutional development orientation of projects. This needs to proceed from recognizing the value of institutionalized management, planning, and research instead of relying on the ad hoc (noninstitutionalized) project unit or special study or task force, especially where these, in effect, debilitate existing institutions or obscure the need for permanent institutions. Development planning for the sector needs to include

institutional development programs designed to bring about the capacity needed to manage the developing system efficiently.

3. *Development of efficient organization and methods.* The detailed review of organizational structures, systems, and procedures to determine the minimum resources needed for efficient discharge or responsibilities of each unit (including staffing levels, funding, and so on) is a continuing obligation in a dynamic institutional setting. It is no longer enough to have a small O and M unit in ministries of finance or establishment ministries. This kind of review is needed at the sector level to help with introducing modernization and adjustment in a systematic, well-planned, and continuous way; hence, small O and M units should urgently be developed for the civil service establishment. Essentially, however, this recommendation is concerned not merely with O and M units of the type that only react to proposals for change but with units that plan and organize change, conduct their own investigations and research, and pilot change and suggest new operational methods well before a situation becomes critical. These O and M reviews may reveal staff redundancies in some units and deficiencies in others, and major adjustments will be needed as new units or activities are created and old ones abolished or phased out and staff are trained or retrained for new roles and redeployed. This kind of adjustment entails costs that should be included in capital investment programs and external borrowing.

4. *Expanded staff training.* A staff-development policy is needed that attends to induction training of all staff and systematic in-service training at all levels and determines what preservice training programs are needed to produce new recruits in the desired specializations. For ministries of education, there will be specific training needs in such areas as educational planning and development, including the management of development programs and projects; selection, procurement, and maintenance of equipment; financial management and planning; and educational administration and study tours and seminars for senior managers, especially to permit intercountry exchanges. Often these sector-specific training needs would require to be supplemented and supported by addressing core ministry training needs (e.g., finance, planning, and civil service establishment).

Certain staff training needs (such as statistics) would best be approached in a wider national or regional context.
5. *Provision of buildings and equipment.* Within the development programs of the ministries, due attention is required to the inadequacy of buildings, furniture, equipment, and vehicles under which the administration now functions. This includes recognizing the need for (i) appropriately designed buildings that take into account growth requirements, (ii) data-processing equipment, and (iii) office equipment and supplies. It also includes a resolution of the urgent transport problem. This requires a fleet of diverse types of vehicles, with the necessary garages, maintenance, and repair services (preferably at the sector ministry level in order to avoid excessive management problems), a stock of spare parts and initial operating costs, and a program of training of drivers and managers in vehicle operation and fleet management and control.
6. *The provision of information resources.* The ministries of education need to be assisted in designing and establishing documentation library, information, and services for themselves at central and provincial levels in the planning and implementation of a program of strengthening the national library service, and in the collection and processing of statistical data on the sector.

Strengthening Management Development

The improvement of training in management and public administration needs to be approached through a variety of means. This involves the following:

1. Support for rationalizing the existing institutional base in management development in the public and private sectors and support for coordinating capacity.
2. Careful selection of training institutions to be developed as centers of excellence, which would include strengthening their capacity for training, research, and consulting work in general. (To begin with, only institutions that are interested in improving their credibility with their clients and in developing a portfolio of programs that could eventually pay their own way should be

selected. One good performance indicator for these programs would be the proportion of the budget of participating institutions being willingly financed by clients in exchange for result-oriented services.)
3. Improvement in both the *range* of programs so as to cover, inter alia, social sectors, sector development programs and development management, and the *quality* of programs, supporting these with the preparation and procurement of appropriate training materials.
4. A program to encourage closer collaboration between public and private sectors in financing management development, the assessment of training needs, and the design, utilization, and evaluation of training programs.
5. Development of public-administration training to cover induction as well as in-service training to provide regular seminars for senior level staff.
6. A program to train trainers not only in instruction techniques but more importantly in how to define needs, to help client set aims, to follow up with clients on the adoption of improvements in their organizations, and to work with clients to publicize successful programs in order to attract managers.
7. A program to train managers of management development institutions. Such a program would include skills in public relations, leadership and staffing, and cost estimation of training and management-development services.

Support for the Management of Vocational Training

The efforts in development of vocational training should continue with intensification of focus on behalf of strengthening institutional capacities to coordinate and manage vocational training in certain respects:

1. establishing coordinating arrangements that give prominence to collaboration among employers, workers, and government in the financing, design, management, and evaluation of vocational training policies and programs and working toward financial autonomy of the system;

2. information and research services for labor-market data, evaluation of experiments, preparation and production of training materials, and low-cost training methods;
3. training of better-qualified managerial personnel and of staff engaged in planning and research, and in equipment selection and maintenance;
4. adoption of career incentives to retain qualified personnel; and
5. exploring the scope for subregional and regional cooperation.

Strengthening Universities

The Bank needs to adopt a new strategy toward universities in Sub-Sahara Africa in which disciplines essential to the welfare of the education sector (as well as other sectors) are strengthened. These disciplines include economics and the social sciences, accountancy or financial management, statistics, architecture, and education management and research. Where applicable, university institutes for business management and public administration should also be included. The aim of such strengthening would be to improve the quality of the graduates by modernizing curricula and equipment and raising the average caliber of teaching and research staff. This would be in order to establish or strengthen research and postgraduate training and to establish or strengthen consulting capacity of the universities in these fields. Essential parts of such improvement would be the upgrading of university library and documentation services and measures to stimulate and support university involvement in research of direct relevance to the resolution of critical national problems.

In all these recommended measures, the relevant UN agencies, particularly ILO, UNESCO, and the Bank, should intensify their assistance to the member countries.

In particular, the Bank needs to take the following measures:

1. Support as a matter of high priority the above efforts in its lending operations and, to this end, agree with each country on a long-term strategy for institutional development and on the need for a series of successive investments, possibly including sector adjustment lending and measures such as financing time slices of agreed sector-development programs in order to permit

fuller realization of institutional objectives. For each lending operation in the sector, therefore, a statement as to the adequacy of administrative and planning resources and capacity for the sector would need to be made as to the existing school system and as to the additional burden of the expansion or improvements envisaged under the project, and any deficiencies noted would need to be addressed, whether within that lending operation or by other specified means.

2. Recruit more appropriate staff (staff with some background in senior management and planning) and train existing staff as needed to upgrade their knowledge of institutional development.
3. Include in its policy and research program efforts (a) to determine, for various sizes of school systems, what constitutes a norm or desirable level funding for administration, whether expressed as an amount or as a percentage of overall sector funding, as well as what is a norm or desirable proportion of national resources to devote to education; (b) to learn more about institutional development in education and training—and use the resources of relevant UN agencies in this—and address such issues as the cost and financing of administration, requirements, and efficiency of administrative decentralization and the cost effectiveness of separate ministries for higher education.
4. Encourage the Economic Development Institute in its policy of training trainers, in its focus on Sub-Sahara Africa, and in establishing collaboration with the International Institute for Educational Planning and other agencies for these objectives.
5. Collaborate closely with relevant multilateral agencies, especially ILO and UNESCO, in regard to national as well as subregional and regional efforts in strengthening education research, planning and management, management development, and the management of vocational training, as well as in promoting the exchange and dissemination of experiences and information.

Problems And Needs Of Institution Building In Management Development And Training

Any discussion of the problems of institutional development in Sub-Sahara Africa in management development and training would need to recognize the peculiar situation of the private sector. In many countries, a clear distinction should be drawn between the large, often foreign-owned enclave operations in mining, forestry, and plantations in various cash crops on the one hand and small scale, largely indigenous entrepreneurship on the other. The first category tends to look after its own management development and vocational-training needs and interacts only marginally with the governments on these. The second category, less well-financed and less well-connected internationally, tends to be slower to recognize the benefits of management development and vocational training, to invest less in these, and to encompass a very wide range of resource levels among its membership. This latter group would ordinarily be far more dependent upon government initiatives and policies in management development and vocational training.

Management Development

Background

During the past twenty years, considerable efforts have been made in most Sub-Sahara African countries to promote management development and training and to improve management in practice. The policy-making circles in these countries have become increasingly aware of problems with the quality of management in many public and private organizations and of the need for remedial measures. Large numbers of management institutes and centers have been established, and a considerable amount of technical assistance has been channeled to this area. Yet the existing institutions are fragile. The programs for managers are frequently criticized by the practitioners, and the real impact of management-development efforts on improving management in practice is not easy to demonstrate. In Sub-Sahara Africa, there have been difficulties in establishing strong public and private institutions that can be regarded as centers of excellence. This has limited the impact and effectiveness of management development and training in these areas. These institutions have not been able to build up a strong reputation, although they do provide a full range of services, such as conducting courses and undertaking consulting assignments. Managers in government and business are, therefore, reluctant to use their services for their strategic problems. They will use them only if their services are provided at little or no cost. Hence, only a few institutions have been exposed to the market test of being required to sell their services and find clients prepared to pay a full price for these services. By its nature, the process of management development is quite different from formal education and vocational training. It is highly diversified and technically demanding, and most of it occurs on the job. A management-development program emphasizes the practical needs of individual managerial positions and of persons holding these positions or preparing themselves for future jobs. It is, therefore, difficult to define what aspects of management development can and ought to be institutionalized at what level and by whom. Views differ on the need to institutionalize management development. One view is that every country and organization should have a clearly spelled-out management-development policy as well as the institutional machinery for implementing this policy. Another view is that it is enough to make certain management-development services and facilities available and to leave individual organizations and managers free to decide whether to use them. In practice, an appropriate institutional framework for management development is seldom defined and its elements seldom clearly identified. A systematic approach is seldom taken, and countries rather proceed case by case, establishing individual institutions or introducing individual institutional measures (such as creating a national council for management development) as needs are recognized.

The relationship between the public and the private sector is delicate. In principle, an institutional framework for management development can serve either one of these sectors or both. In most developing counties, the functions of the government in development also include the provision of institutions and services to the private sector. However, this institutional framework can be effective only if it correctly reflects the needs and aspirations of the private organizations served it the government and the private sector work in harmony toward commonly agreed goals. The efforts made so far in management development have suffered from problems of poor coordination, lack of financial autonomy, deficient staffing, and limitations of mandate and scope.

The European Experience

Even before the founding of the European Community, the idea of a closely knit association of European states had found political expression in a variety of ways. There had been attempts to impose unity by force, notably by Napoleon and Hitler. Napoleon seeking to unite the continent under French hegemony, Hitler to subjugate Europe under the dictatorship of the Third Reich. But there had also been peaceful schemes, especially after the harrowing experiences of the First World War, for a voluntary grouping of states on terms of equality.

In 1923, for instance, the Austrian leader of the Pan-European Movement, Count Coudenhove-Kalergi, had called for the creation of a United States of Europe, citing examples such as the success of the Swiss struggle for unity in 1648, the forging of the German empire in 1871, and the first and foremost the birth of the United States of America in 1789. Then on September 29, 1929, in a now-famous speech before the League of Nations Assembly in Geneva, the French foreign minister Aristide Briand, with the backing of his German counterpart, Gustav Stresemann, proposed the creation of a European Union within the framework of the League of Nations. The immediate aim was merely to promote closer cooperation between the states of Europe, leaving their national sovereignty intact. But all these efforts to peaceful unification failed to make any real headway against the still dominant tide of nationalism and imperialism. Only after Europe had yet again been devastated by way was the disastrous futility of the constant rivalry between nations truly appreciated. Europe's complete collapse and the political and economic exhaustion of the European States, with their outdated national structures, set the stage for a completely fresh start and called for a far more radical approach to the reordering of Europe.[1]

At a meeting of foreign and defense ministers held in Rome on October 26 and 27, 1984, on the occasion of the thirtieth anniversary of the signing of the WEU Treaty, the member states agreed to exploit the existing scope of the WEU on security and defense in order to create a European identity in this field and give greater weight to the European identify in this field and give greater weight to the European voice in the Atlantic alliance.

The characteristic feature of the second group of European organizations is that their structure is designed to allow as many counties as possible to participate. Consequently, it had to be accepted that their activities would not extend beyond the scope of normal international cooperation. Their prime concern is to accommodate countries that are unable or unwilling to become members of an organization endowed with supranational powers, either because of their traditional neutrality—as in the case of Sweden, Austria, or Switzerland—or because of their reluctance to cede any part of their sovereignty.

This group comes under the umbrella of the Council of Europe, which was founded on May 5, 1949, as a political organization. The Statute of the Council of Europe contains no reference to any such goals as federation or union, nor does it provide for any transfer or pooling of areas of national sovereignty. Decision-making power resides solely with a Committee of Ministers, and unanimity is required for all decisions on matters of substance.

Economic and Monetary Policy

The community's founders fully realized that the creation of the common market and the effective implementation of common policies would have to be accompanied by a common economic and monetary policy. It was clear that the establishment of the common market would lead to growing economic interdependence between the member states, making it more difficult for them to pursue their

---

[1] Michael Andre (European Unification, p. 45–49, December 1987).

own short-term economic policy objectives. Conversely, economic and monetary measures adopted by one country would have a considerably greater impact on its partners as economic interdependence grew. It was therefore essential to establish at least some common ground in these policy areas.

However, when the community was founded, no one had sufficient courage to brave the leap forward to a common economic and monetary policy that would lead to Economic and Monetary Union. The member states were not prepared to yield their sovereignty to the community in matters of monetary, budgetary, and fiscal policy. Instead, the common aims of national economic policies were laid down, whereby the member states committed themselves to the goals of full employment, price stability, balance of payments equilibrium, and currency stability. The six founding members also resolved to coordinate their economic policies in close consultation with the community institutions. But responsibility for formulating and implementing economic policy was to remain the sole prerogative of the member states.

It very soon became apparent that the realities of progress in coordination fell far short of expectations. Although it was generally held to be of vital importance for the consolidation of European integration, the great step forward to economic and monetary union proved impossible to achieve.[2]

At the 1969 Hague Summit, the political leaders of the community launched a new initiative for economic and monetary union. The council and the commission were instructed to draw up a timetable setting out the stages for its achievement. A committee was set up under the chairmanship of Pierre Werner, the prime minister and finance minister of Luxembourg, and in October 1970, the committee presented its final report. The Werner Plan envisaged three stages on the road to economic and monetary union, aiming to achieve the final stage ("communalization" of national instruments for economic and monetary control and their use for common ends) by the year 1980. On March 22, 1971, the council adopted a number of decisions, to be effective retroactively from January 1, opening up the way for the first stage of economic and monetary union to begin.

---

[2] Eric G. Freiberg (*Harvard Business Review*, May–June 1989, pp. 85–89).

But as early as April 1973, the commission presented a sobering report to the council on the initial stage. The member states had achieved hardly any progress in coordinating their economic policies. Under the pressure of accelerating inflation everywhere and violent fluctuations on the international foreign exchange markets, they all preferred to seek refuge in unilateral national action rather than to embark on a common course with the prospect to medium-term success. Their political will to submit to a common discipline and to make effective use of the community armory was sacrificed to the desire for short-term gains. Nevertheless, the community endeavored to keep to the timetable for economic and monetary union, with the second stage due to begin in February 1974. However, the attempt failed, and the second stage never got off the ground. Instead, the starting date merely saw the adoption of a number of individual measures to improve and extend the range of instruments available for monetary policy and the coordination of economic policies.

The setting up of the European Monetary System (EMS) in March 1979 gave a new dimension to European monetary cooperation. Its purpose was to create a zone of monetary stability in Europe as free as possible of wild currency fluctuations. It was primarily because of the volatility of exchange rates that European firms had fought shy of undertaking major long-term investment projects in other community countries and had been unable to take full advantage of the common market. With frequent unpredictable shifts in exchange rates, firms found that making broad economic calculations had become little more than a game of roulette, and the stakes were too high for their liking. The EMS seeks to achieve its objective of internal (price) and external (exchange rate) stability by means of a system of fixed but adjustable guidance rates resting on a variety of intervention and credit mechanisms. The obligations imposed on member states by the system and the way in which it operates have led to greater convergence between the economic and monetary policies of the member states, with the result that it is generally held to be a success. Within the system, the ECU plays a central role. (The name has a dual parentage: it stands for European currency unit; at the same time, it also revives the name of a thirteenth-century French gold coin.) The ECU comprises a "basket" of the currencies of the member states, each currency accounting for a proportion, which is determined on the basis of the economic strength of the country in question. The exact value of the ECU in terms of each currency is fixed every day by the commission, and the rates are published in the Official Journal of the European Communities (C series).

The ECU fulfills four functions: it is the reference unit for the exchange rate mechanism, it acts as an indicator to determine when one currency deviates from the others, it serves as a unit of account for transactions under the intervention and credit mechanism, and it is used for setting debts between national monetary authorities. It is also used as the unit of account for the community budget, and all specific external duties, levies, refunds, and other internal community payments are expressed and settled in terms of ECUs.[3]

In private transactions, the ECU offers business, workers, and the ordinary citizen protection against sudden fluctuations in exchange rates. For banking purposes, it already operates as a fully fledged Euro currency, being used for private and business savings and overdrafts, especially by small and medium-size firms and independent operators. The hope is that people will ultimately be able to use the ECU in any member state as an acceptable alternative to the national currency. But this goal is still a long way off, and economic and monetary policies will have to grow much closer before it becomes a practical proposition.

As Europeans head toward 1992, goods and services will no longer be subjected to trade barriers; neither will money. There would even be a Euro-style Federal Reserve Bank. Banks, investment houses, and insurance companies are racing to position themselves for the new Financial European. Some four hundred banks and finance firms across Europe have merged, taken stakes in one another, or devised joint marketing ventures to sell stocks, mutual funds, insurance, and other financial instruments to consumers. Europeans are hoping that these alliances will be both helpful to strengthen the institutions at home and giving many a stage up in global rivalry to the powerful Japan, the United States, and Switzerland, who are firming up their own European campaigns. The European Community's Council of Ministries is considering restricting the activities of some foreign banks if their home countries don't grant European privileges

---

[3] Nan Stone (The Changing Map of Europe, May–June 1989, pp. 92–93).

similar to those foreigners would enjoy in Europe. The European Community's main target is Japan and perhaps the United States. Europeans have been allowed to give out only a tiny share of bank loans in Japan against a 10 percent share for the Japanese in Europe. The United States is vulnerable too because it keeps banks out of underwriting and bars unrestricted expansion across state lines. Most experts see integration coming about gradually. The European Community might make a start by pooling foreign exchange reserves, creating the management of a diverse board of governors similar to the United States Federal Reserve. Many obstacles stand in the way of full integration. The European Community is a long way from unifying its tax structure, which could send massive amounts of funds and jobs to countries offering the safest havens.

Economic Integration

1. The Common Market

    The focal point of economic integration is the common market, in which the member states have combined to create a unified economic territory undivided by either customs or trade barriers. This common market rests on the pillars of four fundamental freedoms: the free movement of goods, persons, capital, and the freedom to provide services.
    First and foremost, it allows capital and labor—two basic factors of production—to develop their potential unhindered. Workers can move freely to seek jobs where demand is higher and wages and working conditions accordingly better. They can settle with their families and go to work anywhere in the community. Firms can produce and sell their goods in free competition wherever suits them best. No member state may give its own nationals preferred treatment over those of its community partners.
    To create this large European internal market—which, with the entry of Spain and Portugal, now has to serve almost 320 million people—the community countries have had to dismantle all manner of trade barriers, harmonize legislation, administrative practices, and tax structures, and extend their cooperation on monetary policy.

In the run-up to the economic deliberations of the European Council in Milan on June 28 and 29, 1985, the commission prepared a White Paper listing all the measures still required for the competition of the internal market and setting out a detailed timetable for their implementation by 1992. At the Luxembourg European Council in December 1985, the heads of state or government endorsed the commission's objective and gave the go-ahead. All the necessary decisions on customs tariffs, freedom of movements and air and sea transport, and the approximation of laws and administrative rules are now scheduled for adoption by 1992.

The prospects for success are good, since it was agreed at the same time that all these decisions—except those on tax harmonization, the free movement of persons, and workers' rights—would be adopted by majority voting, while special temporary arrangements would be allowed for member states that encountered problems in implementing them.

The following sections describe the development of the internal market so far and the current state of progress:

(a) The Customs Union and Free Movement of Goods

The first step in the creating of the common market was to eliminate all the customs duties levied on imports and exports between the member states before the EEC was established. The EEC Treaty laid down a fixed timetable for the gradual dismantling of these internal duties within twelve years. The original Six had no difficulty in meeting the deadline, and the last customs barriers came down in 1968, eighteen months ahead of schedule. The later entrants also successfully met the tight deadlines set for removing their preaccession customs duties and adapted to the requirements of the common market surprisingly quickly.

The elimination of customs duties within the EEC was accompanied by the establishment on July 1, 1968, of a common customs tariff (CCT), setting up a single customs barrier around the entire community for all imports from nonmember countries, with duty normally being levied when goods enter the economic territory of the community.

This was necessary in order to prevent diversion of trade flows. When the community was founded, wide disparities existed between the member states in their rates of external duty.

These were very high in France and Italy, for example, but low in the Benelux countries and Germany. Without a common customs tariff, French or Italian importers could have evaded the high rates at home by taking advantage of the removal of internal duties to import through agents in low-duty countries and then transport the goods to France or Italy. This could eventually have led to the ridiculous situation of a Bordeaux wine merchant getting cheap Spanish corks via Hamburg.

The CCT rates have frequently been adjusted since 1968. This is done either unilaterally, by a decision of the Council of Ministers, or through negotiations between the community and individual nonmember countries or other international organizations, especially within the framework of GATT (General Agreement on Tariffs and Trade). Since 1975, the proceeds from duties form part of the community's own resources and are paid over to it by the member states. The introduction of a common external tariff signaled completion of the first stage of economic integration: the establishment of customs union.[4]

The creation of a large European market on which all goods can be freely traded requires not only the removal of customs barriers but the lifting of quantitative restrictions too. These are designed to protect a country's industries, warding off foreign competition on the domestic market wither by a temporary or indefinite ban on certain imports or alternatively by restrictions on their value or volume (quotas). Measures of this kind are prohibited by the treaties, and this ban has, in the main, been respected by the member states since the expiry of the prescribed transition periods. Intracommunity trade, then, is also free of all quota restrictions.

One obstacle to the free movement of goods within the EEC that still persists is what is known as "measures having equivalent effect" (to quantitative restrictions). These are measures that, though not actual prohibitions or quotas, have an indirect impact on intracommunity trade by making it expensive, difficult, or well nigh impossible to

---

[4] Raymond Vernon (*Harvard Business Review*, July–August 1989).

import or export certain goods. With structural problems in a number of major industries (steel, shipbuilding, textile), rising unemployment, and escalating imports from low-cost producing countries, member states have been increasingly tempted to erect protectionist barriers, thereby excluding other member states' goods from their domestic markets and hampering intracommunity trade.

This is a game at which the member states have shown a considerable degree of invention and imagination. It starts at the frontier, where, despite much simplification, certain formalities continue to cause tedious and costly delays. The pressing need to solve the problems facing freight transport was highlighted by the incidents that occurred at the Italian-French and Italian-Austrian-German borders in the spring of 1984. The Council of Ministers took a major step toward streamlining frontier formalities in December 1984 when it introduced a single document for intracommunity freight to replace a whole series of forms from January 1, 1988. But once across the frontier, goods still face countless bans or restrictions in the form of a vast array of national rules and regulations prescribing—in the interests of health, safety, consumer protection, or fair competition—their exact makeup and labeling. These range from rules on product ingredients and packaging to technical safety and industrial standards. Paradoxically, they succeed in crippling the sale of foreign goods to the advantage of domestic products even though they apply to both alike—the reason being that they vary so widely from one country to another. A clear indication of the extent to which the member states make use of such obstructive measures are the 250 or so complaints that arrive on the commission's desk each year. These the commission investigates, and if it finds the measures in question contrary to community law, the member state concerned is requested under a special formal procedure to amend or desist from the offending rules or practices. If the member state fails to comply with the request, the commission can refer the case to the Court of Justice, whose decision is binding. In this way, a whole range of rules and measures have been rejected by the court as incompatible with community law, so averting more serious problems of free trade between the member states.

The only definitive solution to the problem, however, is to harmonize national regulations—especially the many differing technical standards—and the rules regarding value-added tax and excise. Only then will it be possible to claim that there is genuine free movement of goods within the community. At the same time, this would allow goods inspections between member states to be dispensed with. The main reason for the existence of these inspections (alongside all the other measures already mentioned) is national tax legislation—another areas where considerable disparities exist between the member states as regards the rates charged. This is particularly true of value-added tax and excise duty on mineral oils, spirits, tobacco, beer, and wine. To ensure that less heavily taxed imports that could undercut home products gain no unfair competitive advantage, the difference in tax is levied at the frontier.

(b) Free Movement of Workers

Apart from a few exceptions, freedom of movement for workers within the community is already an established fact. The rights enshrined in the treaties guaranteeing community workers equality of treatment in terms of employment, wages, and other working conditions were comprehensively dealt with in a council regulation of 1968. This enables a worker from any member state who wishes to better his situation to apply for a vacant job anywhere in the community. As regards access to jobs, terms of employment, and working conditions, he must be treated no differently from nationals of the host country. He is entitled to equal pay and equal treatment in the vent of redundancy. In short, he enjoys full equality of rights with local workers.

In addition, he must be given every support as regards general living conditions in the host country. He thus enjoys the same tenancy rights and benefits as national workers, and his wife and children may also take up paid employment or work in a self-employed capacity: his children are entitled to general schooling and can enter into apprenticeships or vocational training on the same conditions as children of local nationals, and in 1958 a community regulation had already guaranteed that a worker who moved to work elsewhere in the community would suffer no disadvantage in terms of social security on that account.

However, the free movement of workers guaranteed by these measures will not succeed fully in practice until the linguistic, social, and cultural difficulties of integrating workers and their families into the working and social life of their host countries are overcome. This requires not only the equality of legal status already achieved but, above all, emergence of a true sense of community among the people of the community, rooted in the basic idea of European unity.

2. Special Trading Arrangements

(a) Association Agreements

Association Agreements establish special links with nonmember countries extending beyond the purely trade aspect to include close economic cooperation and financial assistance. They can be divided into two categories.

Agreements to maintain the special relationship that exists between some member state and certain nonmember countries. The main reason for introducing arrangements for association was to accommodate the special economic links that some overseas countries and territories maintained as a result of their former colonial ties with Belgium, France, Italy, and the Netherlands. Because of the considerable disruption of trade with these countries caused by the introduction of a common external community tariff, special arrangements were necessary in order to extend to them the community system of unrestricted trade. At the time, custom duties on foods from these countries were lifted. Financial and technical assistance is dispensed by the European Development Fund.

Agreements to prepare the way for possible accession or with a view to the creation of a custom union. Association arrangements are also important in preparing for the accession of new members. They form a kind of preliminary stage to accession, designed to help a country that has applied for membership to bring its economy into line with the rest of the community. This approach proved its value in the case of Greece, which obtained associated status in 1962. Another example is the association agreement signed with Turkey in 1964; this too holds out the ultimate prospect of accession.

(b) Cooperation Agreements

Cooperation agreements are less comprehensive than association agreements, their aim being merely to promote intensive economic cooperation. The community has concluded agreements of this kind with such countries as the Maghreb (Morocco, Algeria, and Tunisia) and Mashreq (Egypt, Jordan, Syria, and Lebanon) groups with the Israel.[5]

3. Development Policy

For the community, promoting relations with the developing countries is not merely a question of economic necessity in order to secure its supplies of raw materials and to extend the markets for its goods; it is also a token of solidarity with the less prosperous and poorest countries on earth. This most significant expression of this concern is to be found in the Lome Conventions of 1975, 1979 and 1984, which have formed the basis for cooperation between the community and many African, Caribbean, and Pacific (ACP) countries. Between 1975 and the end of 1985, their number had grown from the original forty-six to sixty-six, reflecting the need to allow the overseas territories that gained their independence over that time to maintain and develop their economic links with the community within a framework of partnership. Under the Lome Convention, exports from the ACP countries enjoy duty-free access to the community market, and quantitative restrictions are prohibited; only in the case of a few agricultural products are there special arrangements. Discrimination is prohibited as regards the right of establishment and freedom to provide services. It is very difficult to comprehend the success of the European common market when there are diverse barriers like currencies and unstructured tax policies. In order for the common market to be very successful, Europeans must develop one national currency, like the United States, thereby alleviating the problem of adjusting interest rates of member countries, due to currency diversity of member countries. As banks,

---

[5] Richard A. Melcher and Jonathan B. Levine (*Business Week*, November 1986, pp. 70–73).

investment houses, and other financial institutions are beginning to merge before 1992, the question then remains: what becomes of the smaller investors? There will probably be no competition for smaller investors, because fewer giant companies will monopolize the marketplace.

The establishment of the European common market will also be very advantageous for the Economic Community of West African States. It will serve as a haven in providing jobs due to Europe's proximity, Africa's cheap labor, and the similarity in currencies.

A Community for the People

Any political system must attend to the needs of the people living under it, and the European Community is no exception. The community endeavors to do this in two ways. First, all measures for economic integration are also geared toward the goal of social progress. The basic freedoms of the common market, for example, encompass not only the economic objective of a large internal market but also the individual freedoms that guarantee community citizens a minimum measure of personal self-realization transcending national frontiers. Second, the community has been able, over the years, to extend its responsibilities to various policy areas that directly affect the social life and well-being of its people. The door to significant progress was opened at the Paris Summit in 1972, when the heads of state or government agreed on the need for a common approach on social and regional policy and the environment and consumer protection. These are the policy areas that we shall look at in this chapter.

The principal instrument of community social policy, however, is the European Social Fund. It was set up with the aim of rendering the employment of workers easier and increasing their geographical and occupational mobility by offering grants or income support for retraining or further training. Since becoming operational in 1960, it has been reformed several times, and its resources steadily increased. This is clearly illustrated by comparing the amounts allocated to it in the community budgets for 1979 and 1983. In 1979, it received a mere 554 million ECU, or 3.8 percent of the total; by 1983, this figure had risen to 1,495 million ECU, representing 6 percent of the total. At the beginning of 1984, the main focus of the fund's operation was reoriented toward a common employment policy. Special emphasis was laid on combating unemployment among young people, with 75 percent of the fund's resources—almost 1,400 million ECU out of a total 1,850 million ECU in 1984—being set aside for this purpose.

Finally, mention should be made of Article 119 of the treaty, which requires men and women to be given equal pay for equal work. This amounts to a guaranteed fundamental right for women workers in the community—a right that they can enforce vis-à-vis their employers through the national courts. In the mid-1970s, women's rights were substantially strengthened by three directives that extended the legal guarantees of equal treatment at work beyond the field of equal pay so as to include access to employment, vocational training, working conditions and promotions, and social security.

Regional Policy

In the preamble to the EEC Treaty, the member states declared their aim of "reducing the differences existing between the various regions and the backwardness of the less-favored regions." The community set about the task with the creation of the European Regional Development Fund in 1975. With the help of the fund, a growing effort has been made to boost investment and create jobs in poorly developed regions through selective assistance for national projects. The long-term aim is to reduce the disparities between the rich regions and the poor—notably those on the extreme periphery, where agriculture is predominant (Southern Italy, Northwest Ireland, Greece), and those largely centered on crisis-hit industries, such as coal, steel, shipbuilding, and textiles.

As with social policy, the resources earmarked for regional policy have been increased substantially over the years, rising from 257.6 million ECU in 1975 (4.8 percent of the community budget) to 2,140 million ECU (7.3 percent) in 1984. The breakdown of Regional Fund spending among the member states for the same year shows Italy at the top of the list with 29.6 percent, followed by the United Kingdom with 27.1 percent; France, 14.6 percent; Greece, 9.7 percent; Ireland, 8.3 percent; Germany, 6.6 percent; the Netherlands, 1.3 percent; Belgium, 0.9 percent; and Luxembourg, 0.6 percent. At the beginning of 1985, the allocation system was reviewed, and it was decided that a more substantial proportion of aid should flow to the neediest regions in Greece, Ireland, Italy, Scotland, and Spain.[6]

Environment and Consumer Protection

The treaties make no explicit reference to environment and consumer protection as one of the community's tasks. The explanation is principally that the threat to the environment and the risks facing the consumer were less readily apparent when the Rome Treaties were signed in 1957 than they are today. It is, however, characteristic of the community—and clear evidence of the dynamic force of integration—that it has been able to adapt its range of policy instruments to suit the changing needs of the time and society.

The community's environment and consumer protection policy was launched at the Paris Summit in 1972, when heads of state or government declared protection of the environment and the consumer to be one of the community's most important and pressing concerns and called for the preparation of action programs to set such a policy in motion. The commission responded by drawing up a series of detailed and comprehensive programs that have been steadily refined and expanded. Originally, the legal basis for this action, as for research and technology policy, was Article 235 of the EEC Treaty, but under the terms of the decisions taken in Luxembourg in December 1985, environment policy has now been given its own place in the treaty. The main areas of progress in environment policy have been the prevention and monitoring of air and water pollution, the disposal of used oil and other wastes, the control of chemical pollution, and the preservation of wild bird species. In the field of consumer protection, a whole series of directives on health and safety have been issued, notably on preservatives and additives in foodstuffs, industrial goods, textiles, motor vehicles, pharmaceuticals, and cosmetics. There have also been important directives on product liability and misleading advertising. Further commission proposals on door-to-door sales and consumer credit are pending before the council.

---

[6]   John F. Magee (Changing Map of Europe, March–April 1989).

But with the rise in pollution levels and the growing risks to be consumer, all these measures are no more than a step in the right direction. Many more comprehensive and, above all, preventive measures must follow. However, promising initiatives often come up against major obstacles because of their implications for other policies (especially competition and social policy). A striking example was the recent controversy surrounding the fitting of cars with catalytic convertors. This merely serves to highlight the need for unrelenting determination to keep sight of the medium-term and long-term objectives.

Common Commercial Policy

Presenting a common front to the world at large, in other words to nonmember countries, is the reverse side of the creation of a unified internal market. It was therefore logical that foreign trade should be an area of common policy. Responsibility for the precise formulation of this policy lies with the community, whose main tasks are to fix and adjust common customs tariffs, to conclude customs and trade agreements, to harmonize measures liberalizing trade with nonmember countries, to plan export policy, and to decide on action to protect trade, particularly against unfair trading practices (e.g., dumping or subsidies). It would be impossible to give a comprehensive review here of all the community's activities in the field of commercial policy. Two aspects, however, deserve special mention.

(a) The Common Agricultural Policy

Agriculture, as one of the "foundations of the community," plays a key role in community policy. It accounts for much of the largest proportion of community legislation and more than two thirds of expenditure under the community budget. There are two reasons why it is such a major concern. First, ensuring the security of food supplies is traditionally one of the main areas of state activity. And the only way to do this is to attain more or less complete self-sufficiency, which means a tendency to overproduce so as to guarantee supplies when harvests are poor. Second, agriculture is a special case among productive sectors, since it is dependent on factors such as climate, soil, and disease, over which man has little control and which often result in major fluctuations in harvests, thus affecting farm incomes. These incomes must be high enough to preserve the family-run farms necessary for self-sufficiency and to prevent such people from leaving the land. In this respect, agricultural policy also fulfills the roles of incomes policy, employment policy, structural policy, regional policy, and population policy.

In view of agriculture's fundamental importance for the general well-being of the people of the community as a whole, the EEC Treaty had to include rules on the establishment and organization of a common agricultural market. However, these were couched in very broad terms so as to permit the existing national control mechanisms to be brought into line gradually.

The main lines of the common agricultural policy were laid down immediately, following the entry into force of the EEC Treaty at a special convened conference held at Stresa in July 1958. The most difficult problem was to incorporate the different national systems in a common system of market organizations so as to create a community-wide market for agricultural products. To start with, all tariff and trade barriers between the member states had to be eliminated. In addition, a common pricing system had to be introduced to guarantee uniform price levels for farm products in all member states.

This involves three types of price, which serve as the main instruments of the common agricultural policy. The system centers on target price, which is the price that community farmers are ideally supposed to receive. This price is fixed every year by the council. If the actual market price for a product drops below the target price as a result of oversupply, the community intervenes in the market to stabilize the situation. The point at which it does so is determined by the intervention price, which is the price at which the intervention agencies set up for this purpose if the member states have to buy up the product concerned in unlimited quantities (marketing guarantee). The intervention system thus guarantees community farmers a minimum price for their products when they cannot earn more on the market, so as to ensure that they receive an adequate income. In order to protect prices within the community and agricultural production as a whole, threshold prices are set. These are minimum prices for agricultural imports into the community.

For many products, they are higher than the world-market prices, because growing conditions in other parts of the world are more advantageous. To prevent the community market from being flooded by cheap imports from nonmember countries to the detriment of European farmers, a levy is imposed to bring import prices up to the threshold level. The levies, like customs duties, are part of the community's own resources, and revenue from them is entered in the budget. Conversely, the community pays agricultural exporters a refund (i.e., an export subsidy to offset the difference between the world price and the community price). This enables community farmers to sell their products on the world market despite the fact that their prices are generally higher.

The cost of operating the common agricultural market is financed through the European Agricultural Guidance and Guarantee Fund (EAFFG). The guarantee section of the fund, which consumes by far the greatest proportion of resources, principally covers the cost of the minimum price guarantee and export refunds. The guidance section provides funds for structural improvements in agriculture. Originally, the fund was financed by the member states directly, each contributing a proportion in accordance with a special scale, but since 1970, it has formed part of the community budget. This, then, is the basic theory underlying the common agricultural policy; it forms a coherent whole that is consistent with the aims and objectives described earlier.

Putting the theory into practice, however, has posed a number of problems. Setting prices that were out of line with market conditions led to surpluses, which, because of the open-ended commitment to buy up products, had to be financed by the community rather than the farmers. This in turn led to the accumulation of large stocks—the much-publicized butter, fruit, and vegetable mountains and the wine lake 00, which entail substantial storage costs and can only ultimately be reduced at best by special sales and at worst by withdrawal from the market (as in the case of perishable products).

It is mainly because of such operations that the common agricultural policy has come in for growing public criticism. However, it would be overhasty to condemn the entire policy simply because of these aberrations and shortcomings and from there, as sometimes happens, to call into question the utility and purpose of European integration in general. The problems are due less to the system itself than to its implementation. Reforms are essential, and proposals have been submitted for measures to reduce costs drastically and to curb overproduction by making farmers bear a greater share of the responsibility and by pursuing a more cautious price policy. The decisions by the agriculture ministers in early 1984, which included placing a limit on the quantity of milk covered by the marketing guarantee and allocating quotas to the member states, point in this direction. But the German veto on the proposal to reduce cereal price by 1.8 percent for the 1985/86 marketing year has once again shown how great national resistance still is.

(b) Competition Policy

The common market for the goods produced by industry and agriculture can operate smoothly only if conditions of competition are uniform. This is the only way to safeguard equality of opportunity for all in the common market and to prevent action that distorts competition by the private sector or by government. One of the community's tasks is, therefore, to create a system to protect free competition within the common market, based on the competition rules laid down in the treaties. These rules prohibit agreements between undertakings to restrict competition and all forms of abuse by an enterprise of a dominant position on the market—for example, imposing unfair prices or limiting production, markets, or technical development; they also ban or place under the commission's supervision national subsidies (State aids) to individual firms or sectors of industry in order to prevent them from gaining an unfair competitive advantage.

The commission ensures that the principles of fair competition are observed in the common market and punishes infringements with heavy fines. Assisted by the Court of Justice, it is also responsible for refining the competition rules so that they are fully effective. The task facing the community—now as in the past—is the laborious one of developing the wide armory of rules and individual decisions necessary to put the established principles into practice.

The Community and Progress toward Political Union

Following the premature demise in the early 1950s of the scheme to establish a European Political Community and the failure in 1954 of the proposed European Defense Community, no further initiative on political union was launched until 1961. At the Bonn Summit that year, the leaders of the Six instructed a committee chaired by Christian Fouchet, the French ambassador to Denmark, to submit proposals for a political charter for "the union of their peoples." In an effort to find a formula that would be acceptable to all, the committee presented two successive drafts—known as the Fouchet Plans. But in the course of negotiations, a stream of amendments and alternatives were put forward, reflecting the divergent views of the member states on the nature of such a union and the form it should take. The differences between them proved quite intractable, and eventually, on April 17, 1962, at a meeting of the Foreign Ministers in Paris, it was decided to suspend the negotiations. This means that for some years afterward, hardly any genuine progress was made toward the political goal of laying the foundations for an ever-closer union among the people of Europe.

Not until the early 1970s was the impetus renewed. Taking up the call for progress on economic and political union made at The Hague Summit in December of 1972 and 1974 proclaimed as their goal the attainment of European Union by the end of the decade. Leo Tindemans, the Belgian prime minister, was invited by his fellow heads of government to submit a comprehensive plan for European Union on the basis of reports presented by the commission, the European Parliament, the Court of Justice, and the Economic and Social Committee. The Tindemans Report envisaged completion of the Union by 1980 by means of

(i) the establishment of economic and monetary union,
(ii) reform of the community institutions,
(iii) the implementation of a common foreign policy, and
(iv) the implementation of common regional and social policies.

This proved too ambitious a goal to be achieved by the proposed deadline. In the last analysis, failure was due to the irreconcilable fundamental differences between the member states on the constitutional structure and institutional reforms that were needed.[7]

European Scientific and Technical Cooperation: Necessity and Virtues

Whatever might appear advisable in other fields, there is at least one idea that no one disputes today: European cooperation in research and technology is a vital necessity. This idea has gradually gained ground in scientific, industrial, and political circles in Europe, all the more readily since modern science is, and is rightly perceived to be, a highly collective venture. It is clear today that in research and technological development, Europe's only salvation lies in systematic and purposeful cooperation.

By coordinating their own efforts, concentrating their facilities and combining their human and financial resources, the European countries can create the conditions that will enable them to make optimum use of their potential.

Scientific and technical cooperation on the scale of the Community of Twelve will, in many fields, supply the necessary "critical mass" below which there is little chance of R and D yielding high-quality results. Through cooperation, full advantage can be taken of the complementary features in know-how, expertise, and training found in Europe so that the whole becomes greater than its parts, and a combined research effort can be made in highly interdisciplinary fields, on topics calling for an intersectoral approach, etc. Cooperation will also allow full exploitation of the potential inherent in the large community market, now close at hand, while at the same time helping to establish it.[8]

Technological Cooperation, Industrial Cooperation, and the Large Market

This theme of the link between Community R and D and the completion of the large market is sufficiently important to warrant a detailed examination of the aspects involved. The completion by

---

[7] John Templeman (*Business Week*, October 10, 1988, pp. 24–28).
[8] Duncan Dowies (Industrial Biotechnology in Europe, 1986).

1992 of a large European market without frontiers, in which people, goods, and capital would be able to move without hindrance, is indeed a challenge to the community; the completion of this large market will be a vital landmark on the road to integration on which the European states took their first steps just after the end of the Second World War and which they have now been following for some thirty years. Obviously, the whole of economic life in Europe will be affected by the forthcoming attainment of the large market. Numerous community policies are therefore involved in this ambitious task. It can be shown, however, that there is a particularly strong link between the theme of the large market and the effort made by the community to promote scientific and technological cooperation in Europe. This link is obvious in two areas: technical standardization and the opening up of public procurement. In both cases, economies of scale are the factor linking up with R and TD. One of the most difficult obstacles that the European industry has to overcome is the ever-growing cost of R and TD activities. The best way to cover this cost is to produce and sell each of the products developed in sufficiently large quantities.

However, technical products in the marketplace are subject to a tighter system of standards than any other category of goods.

This would not matter if a single system were applied throughout Europe, but that is obviously not the case: the national systems of standards in force differ considerably from each other, thus depriving industry in community countries of the benefits of economies of scale.

Aware of the importance of this problem, the community has been working for years to bring differing national regulations closer together. The new approach it worked out in 1986 may be summarized as follows: it is the community's task to lay down essential requirements with which products must comply. The technical definition of standards corresponding to these requirements is the responsibility of the Europeans standards institutions (essentially CEN and CENELEC, with which the community maintains close relations). For example, in 1986, the council adopted a directive on standards for direct satellite television broadcasting.

It has also adopted two decisions on standardization in information technology and telecommunications and on the mutual recognition of terminal systems.

By helping to speed up the European standardization process, this strategy for the completion of the large market obviously creates conditions more conducive to the strengthening of the European industrial competitiveness and, hence, its capacity to invest in R and TD. Reciprocally, the community's effort to promote cross-frontier cooperation in R and TD contributes directly to the success of this strategy, since it is obviously easier to draw up common standards on the basis of research carried out jointly, especially as some of this research has the specific aim of facilitating standardization work.

The walling off of public procurement of markets is a similar problem. The result obviously is to create as many captive markets as there are member states and to make it impossible for European manufacturers to extend their activities to all twelve countries. The value of public-sector orders is considerable: procurement by public departments constitutes 10 percent of the community GDP, or 20 percent if public-sector undertakings are included. Of all public contracts, however, only 2 percent goes to companies located in other member states.[9]

An important point here is that the share of the public-sector orders in some technological areas is well above the average: for telecommunications, for example, it is 25 percent. This shows how important the community's policy of opening up access or public contracts is for European technological development. Here again the community's action in the field of R and TD could not be defined without considering the other dimensions involved in the construction of the large market, an important landmark on the horizon.

A parallel may be drawn here between community initiatives on technological cooperation and recent legal initiatives designed both to promote European industrial cooperation in the widest sense of the term and to create as homogeneous as possible an economic environment in Europe. The former include the concept of "European economic interest grouping," a legal structure equivalent in community law to the industrial cooperation arrangements existing in the national laws of certain countries. The latter include all the directives adopted on company law so as to harmonize the rules

---

[9] Michel Poniatowski (The Technologies, 1986).

applicable to mergers and divisions of companies, presentation of annual accounts, etc.

Closer to and strictly complementary with the community's direct action of R and TD are its initiatives in connection with financial engineering for research and technological development activities. In the technological development process, there is an intermediate stage at which the projects are risky for a normal bank loan. Aware of this gap and the need to strengthen European financial engineering capacity for R and TD, the commission has examined the possibility of creating suitable instruments to finance cross-frontier cooperation projects in advanced technology (for example, the Eurotech Capital companies that would finance projects of this kind by taking a temporary minority holding and the Eurotech Insured guarantee scheme designed to give partial cover for losses resulting from the risk inherent in the investments of Eurotech capital companies).[10]

Coordination

Coordination of institution-building efforts in all sectors, whether supported by the governments or by donor agencies, has been very limited. Too many measures for building institutions and systems in various sectors tend to be undertaken without any coordination with parallel or even competing efforts in other sectors. There are very few multisectoral and multipurpose institutions serving various client groups, making optimum use of scarce resources and employing a critical mass of professional expertise. Instead, every ministry and donor agency tends to promote "its own," even small institution, despite the resource constraints and bleak prospects for surviving without continuing technical assistance. Even the poorest countries of Sub-Sahara Africa have suffered from the proliferation of institutions and governments that are reluctant to take the steps needed to coordinate, merge, or even abolish institutions. Some countries, such as Nigeria in 1973, have established national councils for orienting and coordinating management-development efforts in various sectors. These bodies have proved to be a useful institutional

---

[10] Graham and Trotman (Natural Analogues in Waste Disposal, 1987, pp. 50–58).

arrangement and platform for discussing policy issues and reviewing the experience of various sectors and institutions, but their real influence on management development in practice has remained limited.

Financing and Autonomy

A high, perhaps excessive, dependence on governments has been another prominent feature of the institutional framework for management development in Africa. In most countries, governments have established institutions for training managerial staff in the public sector, including public administration and public enterprises. In only a few cases, such as Nigeria and Kenya, are there independent private institutions providing training and other services to management. As for management-development policies, many governments, such as the government of Mali, have defined policies for public sector training, but little has been done to develop these policies for the private sector. This reflects the fact that, in most African countries, the employers' organizations do not provide meaningful guidance to members for improving management standards and developing managerial personnel or establish services to members on a self-financing basis. For example, these organizations rarely send training consultants to their member companies to discuss training needs and seldom refer inquiries directly to management-training institutions. They generally try to develop their own management-training programs, despite the shortage of training staff. As was discovered in an ILO 1983 survey of forty-two employers' organizations, twelve of which were African, the main reason they give for this is that government-sponsored management institutions offer no training relevant to their needs.

In addition to dependence upon government funding, several efforts depend upon external aid. Because of poor resource planning and follow-up, the quality and quantity of training usually decline with the withdrawal of outside technical aid. Thus, in Madagascar and Mali, the volume of courses in some national training institutions directly relates to the volume of externally financed assistance. The general absence of management-development institutions supported entirely by internal financing deserves study.

Institutions that do not enjoy decision making and financial autonomy lack a high degree of motivation and are not exposed to financial pressures that would stimulate them to make continuous efforts to improve services to clients and to achieve a reasonable ration between the costs of these services and the fees charged. Instead, many heads of institutions, such as in Sierra Leone and Guinea, see the solution in further grants and subsidies, as well as further aid coming from donors, which would enable them to continue delivering their current services, regardless of client acceptance. The total dependence of an institution on a government department means that clients have little influence on the institution that is supposed to serve them. Thus, clients rarely feel a sense of shared responsibility for the development of their management institutions. Typically, in several African countries, both private and public sector clients criticize the attitudes and services of public administration and management institutes but do not feel that they should take any initiative to help these institutes to become more performance oriented and more effective. Experience from other regions shows that without continuous interaction with the clients, and without adapting to the changing needs and demands of clients, management institutes quickly become irrelevant to their environment.

Staffing

Management institutions suffer serious staffing problems. Rarely can they attract and retain competent staff with both an excellent academic background and practical experience since such professionals usually command better remuneration and more challenging work opportunities in private or even public enterprises. The Eastern and Southern African Management Institute (ESAMI), which offers professional salaries about 20 percent higher than the best civil service in the subregion (Zimbabwe), and the Centre de Formation Compatible in Madagascar, which offers important aspects of staffing. Few institutions are fortunate enough to be managed by directors or principals who are effective leaders in the area of relations with the external world and in orienting and motivating the institution's staff. Leadership could perhaps develop if chief institutional administrators were changed less often.

Limitations in Mandates and Scope

The narrowness of approach to management and administrative development used in most cases where policies have been defined has limited the services offered to clients. Training is usually treated as a separate and self-contained activity, unrelated to other measures and activities required to develop and implement practical changes leading to improved organizational performance. For example, some training policies foresee regular retraining or an increase of the total training effort without defining improvements to be made in career planning and development, staff motivation, planning and control procedures, and so on. While effective training can be the first step toward improved performance, if the total effort is confined to staff training only, training produces little practical effect, and managers become skeptical about its usefulness.

On the basis of their broad management-development policies, several countries, such as Cameroon, have included in their national plans some targets for developing competent managerial personnel. However, some management-training projects are inconsistent with the development goals of the countries, and even where some planning takes place, it is rarely followed through systematically. The actual training tends to be determined rather by short-term criteria—and the immediate availability of resources—than by long-term needs and priorities. For example, in Sierra Leone and Zambia, the Institutes of Public Administration and Management can promote only those courses that its small permanent staff can give, even though other and different training courses are urgently needed.

Existing management-training systems do not cater to significant sections of the national need. In Zambia, public service staff is served by an institute of public administration, but no institution provides induction training or newly recruited civil servants. The civil service training college in Sierra Leone has been closed since mid-1983. In Madagascar, where several institutions offer overlapping programs, certain training needs, such as in the management of social sectors, are covered insufficiently. In general, managers in public administration and the modern manufacturing and commercial sector tend to be better served by institutions than managers in sectors such as health, nutrition, food distribution, education, and rural and community development. The importance of accounting and financial management to the efficient investment and control of scarce resources is increasingly recognized. A few countries have established institutions for development accounting practice and training accounting personnel—the Centre de Formation Compatible in Benin, the College of Accountancy in Malawi, the Institute of Financial Management in Tanzania, or the Centre de Formation Compatible in Madagascar. In many other countries, however, facilities for accountancy education and training are quite inadequate, and the governments have not as yet fully recognized the seriousness of the problem.

Certain institutions suffer from mandates and objectives that are vague and ambiguous. In particular, they view themselves as establishments for providing training courses and not as institutions whose ultimate objective is to improve the quality of management and administration in practice. This concept of the mandate affects the choice of intervention methods and the ways in which the services are evaluated. There are examples of institutions that have developed results-oriented services in close collaboration with the clients (JEIP, 1993). Most institutions focus on developing and offering off-the-job training courses of varying duration for various categories of managers and administrators. Consulting and in-plant training have received less attention and rarely exceed 10 to 20 percent of the total volume of work. Research capabilities are weak. Owing to their limited involvement in consulting and research, many institutions lack insight into the day-to-day realities of management and administration in their county and see no alternative to teaching courses transferred from other countries as a rule from those that provided technical assistance.

In order to respond to the real needs of development administration, public-administration training must take a realistic management approach to economic development in each particular country. However, public-administration institutions in Africa rarely provide action-oriented courses in the management of development processes. Too often, these institutions emphasize the laws, the regulations, the administrative process, and the environment and communication techniques (especially written ones). The Ecole National d'Administration et de Magistrate in Cameroon is an example of this kind of institution, despite the good technical level of its current programs.

Institutions with fully adequate physical facilities for teaching, offices, library, reproduction, lodging (where necessary), and meal services are rare in Africa. In many institutions, physical facilities are inadequate, or their development did not keep pace with the growth of the services. Often, insufficient provisions have been made for maintenance and modernization. In some African countries, deterioration of facilities is rapid because of reductions made in appropriation for supplies and maintenance. This seriously affects the quality and scope of the training that they can provide. The situation in Sierra Leone, total volume of work. Research capabilities are weak. Owing to their limited involvement in consulting and research, many institutions lack insight into the day-to-day realities of management and administration in their country and see no alternative to teaching courses transferred from other countries as a rule from those that provided technical assistance.

In order to respond to the real needs of development administration, public-administration training must take a realistic management approach to economic development in each particular country. However, public-administration institutions in Africa rarely provide action-oriented courses in the management of development processes. Too often, these institutions emphasize laws, regulations, the administrative process, and environment and communication techniques (especially written ones). The Ecole Nationale d'Administraton et de Magistrate in Cameroon is an example of this kind of institution, despite the good technical level of its current programs.

Institutions with fully adequate physical facilities for teaching, offices, library, reproduction, lodging (where necessary) and meal services are rare in Africa. In many institutions, physical facilities are inadequate or their development did not keep pace with the growth of the services. Often, insufficient provisions have been made for maintenance and modernization. In some African countries, deterioration of facilities is rapid because of reductions made in appropriation for supplies and maintenance. This seriously affects the quality and scope of the training that they can provide. The situation in Sierra Leone, where the Institute of Public Administration and

Management was provided with physical plant under the Second Education Project, is generally satisfactory.

Management of Vocational Training

This section deals with the problems and needs of institutions or bodies charged with administration of nonformal vocational training. These problems include (a) a background of relatively recent origin of efforts to organize vocational training and the social attitudes that prevail concerning vocational training, (b) the problem of response to labor market requirements, (c) coordination of vocational training, (d) financial arrangements for vocational training, and (e) the scarcity of managerial personnel in this subsector of training.

The need for nonformal training and, consequently, for institutions responsible for formulating and implementing policies and plans for it arises from a demand by the labor market for large numbers of workers with knowledge, attitudes, and skills that are closely matched to available employment opportunities and which, in many cases, cannot be provided by formal education and training institutions. The reasons why the system of formal education and training has not been in a position in many Sub-Sahara African countries to respond to the demands of the labor market for these types of skills are many and varied. The high cost and inappropriateness of many of its programs to the needs of the workplace, its concentration on initial training, its exclusion of adults, and its limitation to those who have achieved certain levels of general education are among these reasons. Public perceptions have contributed to a misunderstanding of its purpose. The formal system in the vocational area is often seen as a consolation prize for those who fail to gain entry into the general education streams of the school system, and there is widespread belief in a guarantee of employment in the public service for all graduates. Changing such attitudes and expectations is difficult, takes time, and requires a change in the conditions that generated these attitudes.

Another major force responsible for the creation of nonformal training systems is the expectation by governments that these can (a) play a role in stimulating economic development (by enhancing the skills of the labor force), (b) help replace expatriates by qualified nationals, and (c) coordinate the various ad hoc training arrangements organized by government and private bodies, thus, maximizing efficiency and avoiding waste. Several Sub-Sahara African countries, for example, have established institutions to manage training during the rapid economic growth period of the 1960s and early 1970s (for instance, the Ivory Coast, Kenya, Madagascar, Democratic Republic of Congo (DRC) and Zaire), while other countries (for instance, Botswana, Cameroon, Central African Republic, and Niger) have created such institutions in the late 1970s and early 1980s, a period of less-buoyant growth.

Present economic difficulties have placed many Sub-Sahara African countries in something of a dilemma. On the one hand, vocational training that does not lead to employment appears to be an exercise of futility that these countries simply cannot afford. On the other hand, there is a shortage of trained, skilled workers and technicians to build, repair, and maintain the assets for sustained economic development.

Four major organizational models of institutional arrangements for managing nonformal vocational training in Sub-Sahara Africa can be identified, reflecting the most common patterns of allocation of responsibility for nonformal training. These place responsibility under the Ministry of Labor, Ministry of Education, another ministry, or in several ministries.

In most countries, institutional arrangements have not had the flexibility needed to adjust constantly to the evolving social and economic environment. The development of such institutions and of the capacity to manage vocational training has been haphazard and not always smooth. Many of the institutions for managing nonformal vocational training are in the midst of a period of transition, searching to break away from old models—often inherited—and to find their own way of planning and implementing cost-effective vocational training that addresses the needs and circumstances of the countries concerned.

It is, as yet, too early, in most cases, to judge how cost effective and efficient these new and reformed institutional arrangements are. For instance, it is difficult to judge whether the schemes, programs, and centers for which they are responsible will attract a sufficient number of potential trainees of high caliber and how smoothly the outputs will be absorbed into employment that contributes to national economic and social development. However, it has been observed that some of the more flexible and efficient national training management arrangements (e.g., in the Ivory Coast and Kenya) offer a range of training schemes at varying levels and duration that go beyond exclusively long-term (about three years) broad-based in-center training. These include, for instance, apprenticeship schemes and sandwich courses, tailor-made courses for enterprises or sectoral development projects, short-term upgrading, updating and retraining schemes through evening courses, advisory services to enterprises to assist them in establishing in-plant training, mobile training units, and skill testing and trade certification schemes.

This variety of training services allows for more rapid adjustment of course content and supply of output to satisfy demands for skilled labor in a rapidly changing labor market and, therefore, generates high returns on investment. However, few of the institutions for managing nonformal vocational training have achieved a sufficient degree of diversification and flexibility (NPC, 1993).

Problem of Response to Labor Market Requirements

An important hurdle to overcome is the lack of reliable data on man-power supply and demand on the basis of which to formulate training priorities, strategies, and activities. Hence, many Sub-Sahara African countries have been unable to adopt a realistic man-power policy and to elaborate such priorities and strategies.

Recognition of the extent to which they share these difficulties has led a large number of Sub-Sahara African countries to pool their national efforts under a regional project sponsored by the Inter-African Centre for the Development of Vocational Training—CIADFOR—with which the ILO is associated. On the basis of work carried out under this project and country studies prepared on the topic, a number of common needs have been identified:

- improve the systems of collecting data needed for a better knowledge of this labor market and of the training systems;
- develop ways to analyze the relationship between training and employment;

- coordinate efficiently the work of the various national institutions involved in economic and social development, employment, and training;
- train national personnel in this field;
- conduct surveys and studies to improve knowledge and understanding of the informal and nonformal sectors.

Present wage structures in many of the countries inadequately reflect the demand and supply of skills in the labor market. This exacerbates the difficulty of adjusting vocational training to labor market needs. Reports of several comprehensive ILO Employment Strategy Missions have concluded that the jobs available in the public sector—in many of the countries the main employer—are, by the inertia of tradition and vested interests, rigidly tied to the amount of education and academic credentials held rather than to the type of education, training, and experience of the individuals and their competence for particular jobs. Consequently, the best among the young have no incentive to opt for careers as skilled workers and technicians and prefer to pursue academic credentials to improve their job competitiveness.

A further deficiency is that vocational guidance, which ideally creates a link between the world of learning and world of work by providing information on available training, further training, and employment opportunities and conditions. It is almost nonexistent in most of the countries under study. Relevant and reliable information is lacking, and the importance of vocational guidance is not always fully understood. Indeed, the main sources of vocational guidance for young people are family and friends and, in some cases, the general school system—sources that are often insufficiently informed of available training, employment, and career opportunities (ILO, 1992).

Coordination

One of the most striking features of vocational training, by comparison with other educational streams, is the fragmentation of its delivery. This is a task that has to be shared among various ministries, national training institutions, and nongovernmental bodies and enterprises. No single body could carry out the myriad of interrelated functions that go into a smooth and dynamic vocational-training system capable of providing the skilled man power needed in all sectors of a national economy. Proper coordination is complex but necessary in order to avoid duplication of effort and waste of resources.

There is great variety of interested parties (sometimes with conflicting views) involved at different levels in assessing needs, formulating policy, and organizing, implementing, and evaluating vocational training. The major reasons for this complexity are conflicting interests and competition for government funds among various ministries and those responsible for management of training, insufficiency of authority to existing national coordination bodies and councils, and the failure of employers and workers, on occasion, to recognize the extent to which training serves their own best interest.

Improving coordination at all levels and among all interested parties will be a major area of concern in the years to come for most countries. At this stage, however, no common approach or pattern of coordination is discernible. Uncoordinated systems are particularly vulnerable to conflicting external assistance. Many cases can be found where different donors, working in cooperation with different ministries and institutions within one country, assist in setting up separate training schemes that either duplicate, overlap, or contradict one another or that do not conform to national standards.

Those responsible for sectoral development and other large investment projects often bypass the national institutions responsible for managing nonformal vocational training. This often leads to underestimation of the potential contribution of human capital and skill development to economic efficiency as well as to training of inferior quality and quantity, which, in turn, results in unsatisfactory productivity levels and low returns on investment. Moreover, there are seldom provisions for the training of man power needed for the smooth operation, repair, and maintenance beyond the actual implementation period of the project. Training within such investment projects is also frequently provided outside the context of national vocational-training systems and institutions. Little consideration is given, in the context of such projects, to the potential benefits of investing in institutional development as an alternative to investing in "one-shot training schemes." Strengthened institutions could deliver trained man power not only for start-up of projects but also for the more permanent requirements of long-term operations, which seem to pose fundamental problems in many Sub-Sahara African countries.

Although figures on costs of and returns to investments in vocational education and training should be used with the utmost caution, it seems clear that vocational-training investments can be quite profitable. In the Sub-Sahara African context, therefore, the need is profitable. In the Sub-Sahara African context, therefore, the need is to utilize existing vocational-training capacity fully, develop the training potential that exists, and explore and utilize low-cost training schemes. The search for low-cost training schemes and methodologies is a trend common to many of the training institutions. Research, experiments, and pilot projects in this field are being carried out almost everywhere in Sub-Sahara Africa, with or without external assistance. However, there is very little information to the results achieved. There is a good case for the close monitoring of such results, possibly through a regional effort, in order to establish a flow of information among the countries that could assist them in reproducing successful experiences whenever possible and in avoiding pitfalls. A prerequisite of this international cooperation and coordination, however, will be a national capacity to design, monitor, and report upon the various experiments.

The Financing of Training

In most of the countries under consideration, governments have traditionally had to assume a large share of the responsibility for financing the management of the nonformal vocational-training system because enterprises either were unable to finance such training or were unaware of their stake in training. Employers' and workers' organizations, struggling with immediate economic problems, tend to neglect longer-term needs, such as training, and to view it as an expense rather than an investment. Recent legislation, however, shows that many of the countries are searching for a more equitable distribution of the financial burden. Several countries have established levy/grant systems of financing, which can provide considerable impetus to training activities. Indeed, as experience in industrializing and industrialized countries has shown, the participation of employers in the financing of training invariably leads to their greater involvement in the development of training policies and programs, and any financing system should be designed to encourage this. The problem in most Sub-Sahara countries is that the number of enterprises that can contribute to the financing of the management arrangements is small. There appears to be a relation of cause and effect between the source of financing of agencies established to manage nonformal vocational training and their management style and the type of training they encourage. Those financed entirely from government budgets tend to be structured and behave like public bureaucracies—to concentrate on long-term training provided in centers, which closely resembles formal vocational and technical education provided under the Ministry of Education. In Sub-Sahara Africa, employers' and workers' representatives are seldom involved *de facto* in the various stages (Psacharopoulos, G., 1984).

Those agencies financed by a mixed system—government and private sector contributions—tend to be answerable or accountable to the groups they are established to serve, thus securing the active participation of employers in all activities. The activities they carry out tend to be more diversified; and the training they encourage is highly flexible in duration, location, and the methodologies used. These agencies are more to be found in Latin American countries. Extremely few Sub-Sahara African countries have been able, so far, to foster this type of institution.

Even with mixed financing arrangements, however, the heavy initial investments in training facilities and equipment needed in building up a nonformal vocational-training system and its management arrangements would normally require financial contributions from governments initially or through external financing. This heavy initial financing need not become a permanent feature. As training systems become increasingly credible and accountable to their customers, these latter are usually willing to contribute to financing these institutions as well as to participate at the levels of planning, implementation, and evaluation of activities. In turn, the participation and commitment of all concerned provide a good guarantee that training would remain on target with actual employment opportunities and development objectives. So far, very few of the countries of Sub-Sahara Africa have training systems that enjoy sufficient credibility to attract the wholehearted participation and commitment of their customers.

Managerial Personnel

The availability of qualified managerial personnel is an essential prerequisite for the efficient planning, organization, implementation, and evaluation of training. In the view of some, managing a training system has more in common with managing a factory than with operating a civil service department. It has all the elements of conducting a teaching establishment, including the purchase, operation, and maintenance of capital equipment and consumable supplies, often involving very large expenditures. A further feature is the need to keep in regular touch with the "customers"—the employers—in order to obtain maximum job opportunities for graduates. The types of managers needed are in extremely short in Sub-Sahara African countries and tend to be lured into lucrative jobs either at home or abroad. Most managers of training systems in Sub-Sahara Africa tend to come from the ranks of civil servants in the ministry primarily responsible (education or labor) or the ranks of technical school directors. In the light of this situation, training, further training, and updating of managers is an area requiring urgent attention, particularly if continuity and efficiency in the management of training systems are to be ensured. Many of the countries do not have the facilities for training and further training of this type of management staff. Because of the relatively small numbers of personnel needed at these levels and at the same time because of their vital importance for the development of the systems, most of the smaller countries may consider training abroad (overseas or in the region) a cost-effective proposition. In such cases, however, no effort should be spared to retain such staff in the positions for which they have been trained by offering them acceptable salaries, working conditions, and career possibilities.

A further problem is the difficulty in finding personnel qualified to carry out development tasks and to carry out research of relevance to vocational training: assessing training priorities and requirements and developing plans and strategies to satisfy them, developing curricula and teaching materials, keeping abreast of alternative teaching and learning methods, and designing and testing them, and continuous evaluation and feedback. Because of the applicability of such research to groups of countries, there is a strong case for pooling resources at the regional level and so keeping costs at a minimum. Some promising regional activities have already been launched under the aegis of CIADFOR; these experiences suggest that technical cooperation among developing countries (TCDC) is a cost-effective way to researching and solving some of the common problems in the field of vocational training as well as exchanging of information and experiences in this field.

All Sub-Sahara African countries recognize the nonformal training that closely responds to skill needs in the economy and can greatly contribute to improving services and enhancing productivity and product quality in industry and agriculture. Many of the countries have decided to establish services responsible for planning, coordinating, organizing, monitoring, and evaluating such nonformal training. However, in the low-income countries, the strength of these services is negligible, and these countries, along with the middle-income countries, will require considerable assistance in strengthening these services.

The development of the capacity to manage training systems required heavy investments over relatively long periods of time—before adequate levels of self-reliance can be achieved. Under present circumstances, it is impossible for most Sub-Sahara African countries to finance entirely the development of their training management capacity. External finance and the provision of international and regional expertise for the solution of some of the major problems could, therefore, greatly enhance and accelerate the process of institutional development.

Among the more serious challenges faced by the management of training systems in Sub-Sahara Africa are the lack of adequate buildings for vocational training, the shortage of equipment, use of equipment that is inappropriate to the conditions in the workplace, the poor maintenance of buildings and equipment, inadequate provision of training supplies, and the underutilization of installed training capacity. This places a premium on the personnel who can make a convincing case for adequate funding of vocational training, who can plan and monitor the procurement of appropriate types and amounts of buildings and equipment and devise related maintenance policies and systems, and who can monitor the utilization of buildings, equipment, and supplies.

Conclusion. The provision of efficient and effective management for vocational-training systems will require measures to be taken to (i) improve information of labor market and training needs, (ii) formulate national training strategies and priorities with the participation of all concerned, (iii) coordinate the various bodies involved in delivering training, (iv) establish realistic financing arrangements, (v) render existing training institutions sufficiently responsive to changing skill requirements, (vi) provide adequate physical plant as may be needed, and (vii) ensure that training institutions are adequately staffed with qualified managers and teaching staff.

Experience In Institutional Development

(a) The Experience of ILO

Management development. The ILO has been assisting the developing countries to train managers, improve management practice, and build appropriate systems and institutions for management development since 1952. The field activities started in Asia, the Middle East, and Latin America, but over the last twenty years, most projects have been undertaken in Africa. Fieldwork has been oriented and supported by research and program-development activities carried out by the Geneva-based Management Development Branch, in close collaboration with institutions in member states, both industrialized and developing.

In the sectors of management and administration, both public and private, the ILO has been only one of the agencies involved in technical assistance. Many projects and programs (including the establishment of new institutions and the building of their physical facilities) were undertaken without ILO participation. Perhaps the most significant experience concerns the overall pattern of technical assistance of African countries in institution-building in various sectors. It has been most difficult to overcome sectoral barriers at the national level and to coordinate efforts among donor agencies. The growing determination to coordinate technical assistance is a very recent phenomenon, and many past errors in institution building are due to the fact that donors were not prepared or not able, for technical reasons, to harmonize their efforts with other donors.

Drawing from the lessons of past experience, the ILO Management Development Programme has oriented its technical cooperation activities in Africa in four main directions.

Drawing from the lessons of past experience, the ILO Management Development Programme has oriented its technical cooperation activities in Africa in four main directions.

Firstly, ILO seeks to examine the institutional framework, develop policies and plans, and suggest measures for rationalizing the national networks of institutions. This has included national surveys of management-development needs—programs and institutions in countries such as Sudan, Zambia, Benin, Malawi, Nigeria, and the member countries of the CEAO. In this area, however, work has hardly started and will need to be expanded in the years to come.

Secondly, ILO attempts to improve the performance and increase the impact of management-development institutions and programs. In many cases, this implies profound changes in the attitudes and work methods of the institutions. Institutions are assessed in undertaking, in close collaboration with their clients, a self-diagnosis of their performance, and in developing action programs for applying more effective intervention methods and reorienting activities toward priority problems experienced by clients. Particular emphasis is placed on the development of consulting services and of research into local management practices and problems. A major objective is to increase the autonomy of the institutions and their ability to finance an increasing portion of their expenses from their income earned by selling services to clients. Field assistance in these areas has been supported by producing technical guides for institutions covering topics such as how to manage a management institution, how to do management consulting, and how to carry out research. Guides on further aspects of operating an effective institution are in preparation. Since institutions in developing countries need to be assisted in making management training available to large numbers of people for a relatively low cost, training materials are being developed that meet these criteria. For example, so-called flexible learning packages have recently been developed in several subject areas. Programmed texts in financial management and marketing have been developed and widely distributed. A major package on supervisory development has also been distributed.

Thirdly, increased attention is being paid to the needs of certain important sectors where management development formerly lagged behind the manufacturing, trade, and public-administration sectors. In the past five years, ILO has intensified assistance with the design and introduction of new types of sectoral programs in construction and small contractor development, road transport, food distribution, environmental management, rural project management, and eater supply. In all sectors where this is appropriate, particular attention is paid to the need to develop viable small enterprises based on local entrepreneurial talent. Entrepreneurship development and enterprise creating programs have been started in several countries, including, for example, Uganda, Kenya, Lesotho, Malawi, Gambia, and Congo. On the other hand, other conceptual and fieldwork has been undertaken to assist public enterprises, including public utilities, in devising and implementing systematic programs for performance improvement. A guide to planning for improved enterprise performance was published, as well as a new guide for performance improvement and management development, and public enterprise is under preparation.

Fourthly, ILO assists in encouraging and facilitating cooperation among management institutions at subregional, regional, and interregional levels and provides technical support to networks of institutions (as distinct from projects working with one institution only). The methods used include collection and circulation of information, helping institutions to know one another better, and to start cooperating, support to specific cooperation actions involving groups of institutions, support to subregional and other networks, such as associations established by the institutions themselves, and the development of technical guides and training materials that are of interest to the wide public of management institutions. This activity is supported by an UNDP interregional project and directly involves a number of institutions from both industrialized and development countries. The Economic Development Institute of the World Bank provides active support to this effort. ILO also cooperates directly with several regional institutions helping them to develop their services in support of national management-development programs and institutions rather than competing with them. This has included, for example, cooperation with the Eastern and Southern African Management Institute (ESAMI) and preparatory assistance to the Central African d'Estudes Superiors en Gestion (CESG), whose establishment is being prepared by the DEAO with World Bank support.

Management of vocational training. The long history of the ILO involvement in vocational training within the wider framework of all other aspects of labor (including, for example, employment, conditions of work, safety and health, labor standards, and sectoral activities) and the experience it has accumulated in this field have enabled it, over the years, to enlarge the scope of its training activities. Today, it carries out a wide range of conceptual and operational vocational-training activities aimed at all levels of vocational skill for all sectors of the economy through its field structure at headquarters, at the International Centre for Advanced Technical and Vocational Training in Turin, and through the three regional centers (Asia and Pacific Skill Development Programme, APSDEP; Inter-African Centre for the Development of Vocational Training, CIADFOR; and the Inter-American Vocational Training Research and Documentation Centre, INTERFORE).

The growth of the program, however, has not followed a straight path. The program has often been recast to take account of changing environments, the economic and social and policy priorities of the countries, shifting relationships between and within states, and new thinking on objectives and ways of achieving them. For these reasons, and because of the tripartite structure of the ILO, its activities in the field of training have always taken into account the many facets of the world of work in which they take place.

Operational activities started after the Second World War and reflected the concern of a few independent third-world countries to expand their training programs beyond the technical and vocational schools. They were interested in systems of training similar to those in the industrialized countries, particularly those which could respond quickly to urgent man-power training needs. However, the institutional and legal infrastructures for vocational training outside the school system were often nonexistent. This was the case in the majority of developing countries, with the exception of a number of Latin American countries, where institutional arrangements for managing training had already been established.

Needs changed very quickly in the period just before and after the independence wave of the 1960s. Shortages of qualified personnel were acutely felt in all the developing countries, *inter alia*, to replace expatriates. Capacity and willingness of employers in these countries to provide training were quite limited, while the few vocational and technical schools were in no position to meet the qualitative and quantitative needs of the economy. Consequently, the need for government intervention to provide training through adequate institutions became apparent. For the ILO's technical cooperation, this can be characterized as the "institution-building period," which started timidly during the second half of the 1950s, gained momentum during the 1970s, and reached its peak early in the 1970s. Such projects were characterized by large groups of experts, fellowships, and significant equipment components.

A recent study revealed that authorities interviewed in many developing countries felt that the ILO has had a great influence and, in some cases, has been instrumental in establishing national vocational-training institutions and in training the national staff to manage them. Some remarked that, in only a few years, their national institutions and systems had achieved a privileged position in the development of vocational training and that this would not have been possible without the assistance of the ILO's technical cooperation projects. These institution building and strengthening projects have helped in devising national policies and strategies, in setting up and developing vocational-training infrastructures, and in drafting legislation.

While almost all countries were particularly satisfied with this type of technical cooperation, projects that set out to establish the initial infrastructure for vocational training were particularly difficult, hampered by a great variety of problems, and required more time and money than had been estimated at the outset. These were usually "phase 1" projects with ambitious objectives, such as defining national vocational-training policies, establishing the required legislation, setting up and manning the national vocational-training institutions, structuring the various administrative services, initiating instructor training schemes, and starting vocational-training operations for a selected number of basis occupations.

Because such projects are usually pioneering in many respects, they have to solve problems such as the coordination of existing (very often unrelated) training activities under the responsibility of various bodies. They also have to cope with difficulties in determining responsibilities, inadequate budgets and allocation of funds, recruitment and training of management personnel for the national training body, and the provision of adequate physical facilities. In general, it has not been possible to establish a self-sustained management institution for vocational training or infrastructure in any country in just one project phase. Such projects tend to be extended into second, third, and even fourth phases to achieve acceptable self-reliance of the national training-management institution. While during the phase 1 of such projects, it is usually possible to carry out labor market surveys and training needs assessment, as well as to lay the foundation for future action, the actual work and impact on a national scale is achieved at later stages. Thus, it is, as a rule, during the second, third, and fourth phases that ILO has assisted institutions to:

set up trade standards and skill testing and certification schemes,

- launch training within enterprises and apprenticeship schemes with the support of enterprises,
- increase the volume of training,
- establish schemes for instructor training and upgrading,
- extend training to cover rural areas and the informal sector,
- decentralize training activities to other regions of the country,
- implement training for sectoral development,
- start training operations for special groups of the population,
- devise vocational guidance systems,
- determine evaluation procedures, etc.

ILO experience also shows that the support and commitment of government, employers, and workers to institutional development projects tended to be firmer after the early stages of such projects, when concrete results became more apparent.

Traditional cost/benefit analysis cannot be applied consistently to training projects, particularly to the institutional development type.

Furthermore, calculations of numbers of people trained divided by the cost incurred will not give an accurate measure of the efficiency achieved. There is obviously a case for discarding some of the "non-profit making" attitudes in favor of more competitive and cost-analysis-oriented thinking in project development and implementation. However, it should not be forgotten that projects that set out to establish a training infrastructure and to change attitudes toward human-resources development carry a high price tag that it is wise to pay, not only on social and political ground suit but also for long-term economic reasons. Furthermore, once management arrangements are more or less firmly established, other training projects (national or international) tend to become increasingly efficient because of the management support they receive.

An analysis of the ILO's past technical cooperation activities has shown that requests for technical cooperation in the field of vocational training bear some relationship to the state of development of the country asking for cooperation. The least developed countries (which is the case for many of the Sub-Sahara African countries), which usually lack strong training institutions and infrastructure, tend to seek exploratory missions or pilot projects. As a general rule, these are following by comprehensive institution building and strengthening projects that have more than one phase and extend over long periods of time. Within this process, operational activities also tend to follow a certain order. This starts with the organization of a national institution responsible for training, including the necessary legal framework, the setting up of pilot training centers and in-plant and apprenticeship schemes, and a gradual diversification of the skills taught and the teaching methods used. Only when a certain degree of development of the vocational institution and infrastructure has been achieved—aside from emergency situations—do governments tend to make requests for projects such as cooperation in designing training programs that are very specific to skills and sectors of the economy, target groups, and purposes. Although the chronological order tends to be the same, the end products do vary in accordance with national characteristics and development requirements (ILO, 1992).

ILO's experience shows that successful institutional development projects have a number of factors in common—strong commitment by the government to the management of vocational training, the relevance of such conditions, and the availability of adequately qualified international national counterpart personnel.

During the 1970s, a number of African countries requested cooperation from the ILO to assist them in their efforts to improve technical cooperation among developing countries (TCDC) in the field of training. In response to these requests, the African Centre for the Development of Vocational Training (Centre Interafricain Pour le Developpement de la Formation Professionnelle—CIADFOR) was founded on July 1, 1978. CIADFOR has been carrying out a program that enables its members—about twenty countries at the present time—to cooperate in the field of vocational training. CIADFOR's structure comprises a Ministerial Conference responsible for policy guidance that meets once every two years. It also comprises a Technical Committee (composed of government representatives in charge of vocational-training management and of representatives of employers' and workers' organizations), meeting once a year and responsible for the programming and supervision of program execution. A secretary general appointed by the Ministerial Conference is responsible for the submission of proposals to the Technical Committee. An executive director, appointed by the director-general of the ILO, is responsible for program execution and the budget.

Apart from financial contributions provided by the National Agency for Vocational Training (ONPF-Ivory Coast) and the ILO, CIADFOR relies, to the utmost extent, on the contributions in kind, which the members put at its disposal. CIADFOR has been conceived to fill a gap that has been felt over the years, namely to train policy makers to enable them to discharge their functions more efficiently. With this in mind, the objectives of CIADFOR are the following:

- Developing and fostering the exchange of information, experience, expertise, and training materials;
- Training of policy makers responsible for the planning, execution, monitoring, and evaluation of vocational-training institutions, systems, and programs; and, in general,
- Enhancing cooperation among members of CIADFOR

CIADFOR's performance is very much appreciated, as manifested by the interest of its members in taking on the responsibility for executing projects and contributing within the framework of their vocational-training institutions. The English- and Portuguese-speaking countries in Africa have manifested their interest in actively participating in the work of this regional center. The ability to accommodate an expansion of the coverage of CIADFOR's membership in the future will largely depend on whether additional funds can be obtained for this purpose.

(b) The Experience of UNESCO

Institutional development in education was always an important component of UNESCO's activities, although the term "institutional development" was rarely used and the development and strengthening of institutions was considered rather as a useful and desirable by-product than as the main objective.

Technical assistance in education planning, administration, statistics, curriculum development, and so on was always and still remains an important part of UNESCO's activities. For example, in the 1960s and early 1970s, the education sector in UNESCO paid great attention to creating and/or strengthening of Higher Teacher Training Colleges (Ecoles Normales Superieures), Faculties of Education and National Pedagogical Institutes (Instituts Pedagogiques Nationaux) in Sub-Sahara Africa and in other regions. The objective was to provide a sufficient supply of trained teachers for secondary schools and to create national capacity for teachers for secondary schools and to create national capacity for curriculum development and education research; although this effort leads to building institutions, the term "institutional development" can hardly be found in any of the corresponding project documents. The main objective was the activity to be performed, the institutional aspect being considered as a necessary and welcome by-product. Activities in this field still continue (such as in the Ibadan University Faculty of Education Management in Nigeria) but on a far smaller scale because, in most African countries, these institutions already exist and have become an integral part of the national educational system. The effort in this field can be considered a success; although, obviously, a 100 percent success of any particular project is extremely rare, and many projects experienced problems and difficulties due to a series of reasons that will be discussed later.

For more than twenty years, since 1963, the International Institute for Educational Planning established by UNESCO has conducted training courses for educational planners. Most of the trainees, according to recent estimates (80 percent according to a tracer study carried out in 1973), still work in educational planning and management. The mission found ex-trainees of IIEP in important positions in all countries visited.

Most of the technical cooperation activities of UNESCO were financed by UNDP; however, within the last ten years or so, the UNDP financial crises reduced the funds available for most countries. The share of total funds from this source going to UNESCO from projects assisted by the bank have declined. Thus, in recent years, the total amount of assistance (from regular budget and extra-budgetary sources) has declined.

With the decline in available funding for technical cooperation activities, the composition and character of UNESCO assistance is changing to less costly but efficient modes. There is a clear tendency to move away from long-term assignments (two to five years or more) where experts, in many cases, were, in fact, filling staff positions in ministries of education, to short-term (two weeks to three months) assignments, which focus on organizing and conducting training programs, courses, seminars, workshops for senior staff already in service, and also on assisting national staff to prepare various studies, such as costing and feasibility of an educational reform, manpower assessment, financing of education, and preparation of a new programs of the ministry. Parallel to this trend, UNESCO Technical Assistance is becoming more specialized and covers subjects such as school mapping, university management, cost analysis, and so on.

The switch to shorter, highly specialized and more precisely timed interventions is proving to be successful and contributes more effectively to institutional development than did the previous pattern. Short-term interventions by appropriate specialists do not replace national staff but tend to promote their knowledge in specialized fields and their in-service training. Experts on long-term assignments very often just occupy a vacant position in the national structure. Upon completion of their contracts, they leave with their knowledge and experience, leaving behind their position vacant again—sometimes frozen or abolished in the next round of budget restriction.

Technical assistance—whether it is a separate activity or a component of a major project—contributes to institutional development only when it leaves some additional expertise or improved systems or procedures behind upon completion of the project. This is best done my training counterparts as part of the project activities. Most projects (especially those financed by UNDP, but less so in the past those financed by the World Bank or by regional development banks) require that full-time counterparts be formally appointed by the governments to work with the expert. However, in many cases, the appointment of a counterpart is a very slow process, and one to two years of the presence of the expert may be lost for training. It has also happened that the counterpart was finally appointed one month before the expert's contract expired. In other cases, counterparts change so often that there is no time to train them properly. Counterparts trained by the experts were often appointed to posts other than those for which they were trained. In one country in Sub-Sahara Africa, the UNESCO expert in educational planning and administration trained four counterparts; only one of them remained in educational planning. The three others have been appointed to positions such as director of customs, director of the National Coffee Board, and ambassador. The same is often the case with persons sent for training abroad within the project; their appointment to the project is not a general rule. While this is not a loss for the country (and it may well be that in the new nonproject position, the person's qualification and capacity are better utilized), it is a loss for the project and for the activities that the project was designed to assist.

A recent, and so far successful, initiative is the Network of Educational Innovation for Development in Africa (NEIDA), which aims at improving the internal efficiency of education systems by the consolidation and extension of educational research. Conceived as part of technical cooperation among developing countries, assistance is given by UNESCO to regional and subregional cooperative programs for educational innovation. This assistance helps member states to intensify and extend direct exchanges of information, experience, and personnel between research institutions in the various fields of major interest defined by their participants in the programs. It also helps launch cooperative research and development activities and encourage wider application of innovations that have already been tested. At the worldwide level, the International Bureau of Education (IBE) in Geneva—among other activities—sees to the international circulation of information about innovations tested in these networks.

Given that institutional development is a long-term process and that the implementation of a project financed by external assistance is a short-term undertaking (four to five years), it would be unrealistic to expect in all cases to create and consolidate an institution within a project. Some follow-up, for example, in the form of a subsequent project, which could include as one of its components some continuation of the support to the institution created in the preceding project, is usually needed. Several technical assistance projects in which UNESCO was involved in Sub-Sahara Africa had to be discontinued before their completion because of financial problems of the UNDP and their objectives were, thus, only partially fulfilled (World Bank / UNESCO, 1992).

The experience of UNESCO suggests that project design in institutional development needs to pay particular attention to the capacity of the government to meet the investment and recurrent costs involved. This may include ensuring that provisions be made in the project and in follow-up projects for supplies and materials to render the institutional development objectives attainable. Institutional development project design needs to take into account the intricacies of the local situation instead of simple transferring or imposing foreign models and standards poorly adapted to local needs and realities. It needs to involve national expertise and national institutions sufficiently in the process of project identification, design preparation, and implementation if the commitment of the national authorities is to be secured. Nevertheless, there are risks inherent in changes of national officials, which may entail changes in priorities.

(c) Bank Experience in Education Lending

Some one hundred projects were financed by the Bank in the education sector in Sub-Sahara African countries over the period

FY64–84. Fifty-eight of these projects had been completed by March 1985. An analysis of project design in this group of projects reveals patterns of amount and distribution of proposed investments over time and priorities regarding both the areas of the education system selected for support and the means selected to achieve institutional development. Experience with implementation in regard to the completed projects highlights the peculiar vulnerability of institutional development components and the need for more consistent attention to these aspects of projects. In addition, the experience in the five selected countries provides an insight into patterns of behavior in both the design and the implementation stages.

Project design. In the 1960s, the Bank generally left institutional development and software to be financed by bilateral and other agencies. With the broadening of policies in the later 1970s to include financing for these areas, eighty-five of the eighty-seven projects approved in the 1970s and 1980s included institutional development. The average cost of institutional development components rose from US$2.7 million per project in Eastern Africa and US$1.8 million in Western Africa in the 1970s to US$3.4 million and US$6.2 million, respectively, in the 1980s. In Western Africa, roughly 18 percent of total project cost over the period FY64–84 was attributable to institutional development, while in Eastern Africa, this proportion was 11 percent.

The principal areas of institutional development assistance were project management (in 72 percent of the projects approved)—mainly for the purpose of ensuring smooth project implementation—and planning related items, such as educational or man-power planning (64 percent), studies and research (53 percent), and evaluation (31 percent), addressing weaknesses or deficiencies in information in areas vital to the identification of future projects. Thus, there has been a clear preoccupation in these projects with the vigor of the Bank's lending program rather than with institutional development per se.

On a significantly lesser scale, assistance was channeled to technical aspects of educational management (mainly textbooks in 38 percent of projects and curriculum change in 35 percent of projects) in support of qualitative improvements in the schools. Even less attention was devoted to examinations, educational broadcasting, and school supervision.

The broad area of administration also received relatively little attention—central and district management in ministries of education being assisted in 31 percent of projects, financial management in 18 percent, and personnel management in 9 percent of projects. Management training was assisted in 32 percent, and the management of vocational training was in 28 percent of the projects.

The means adopted to achieve institutional development was overwhelmingly that of providing expert services—in 85 percent of the projects and indeed in 35 of the eighty-seven projects, FY70–84. Provision was also made for fellowships (48 percent of projects), physical plant (46 percent of projects), and support of operating costs (30 percent of projects).

A striking deficiency in project design for institutional development has been the lack of emphasis on long-range training for the kinds of specialists required in educational development—architects, evaluators, researchers, accountants, procurement and equipment specialists, and economists, as well as the paucity of support for Sub-Sahara Africa universities, especially in economics and the social sciences and the "strategic disciplines" noted above (paras. 2.11–2.17). The frequent criticisms in appraisal reports of the high enrollments in law and the social sciences has tended to obscure (a) the serious problems of quality and obsolescence, which were developing in a rapidly evolving area of knowledge essential for good social and economic planning, and (b) the need to help develop local research and consulting capacity in these fields within universities and university research institutions.

Project implementation. The implementation experience of these institutional development components goes a long way to amplify the degree of importance attached to them by Bank and the countries and the thoroughness and effectiveness of their design and preparation.

Neither in project management nor in planning have strong and effective units emerged on the scale that one would have expected. The extensive *project-management* efforts have had disappointing results. Perhaps, this is largely because of priority having been accorded to project implementation. The lessons of these efforts are that there should be more systematic efforts at promoting local participation in implementation, that permanent posts with adequate salaries should be provided for local staff, and that larger training programs are needed. In the case of *educational planning*, the efforts appeared quite inadequate for long-term strengthening of the function. In some cases, the emphasis was placed on preparing a plan rather than preparing planners and reinforcing a planning mechanism. On occasion, even this limited objective was replaced by sector or subsector analyses. Only in very few cases did a strong planning function develop. The studies/research items proved to be extremely vulnerable. There was little country commitment to them. Many were deleted, not done, or changed substantially. Some were of limited value as they were seen as having been conceived and conducted by foreigners.

In the technical aspects of educational management, there have been some good results, especially in curriculum development, but there were poor results in educational broadcasting, where follow-up by the Bank was weak or lacking.

The components designed to strengthen central and district administration and management training were generally among the most useful and successful. The efforts to bring together employers and government ministries in the management of vocational training were particularly successful in Ivory Coast, Senegal, and Liberia but less so in Benin and Congo.

The means adopted to effect institutional development appeared to be an important determinant of success or failure. Buildings proved valuable, although there appears to have been tendency to underestimate the requirements. Fellowships tended to be too few or absent. The use of experts has been problem ridden. Strong reactions against their high cost have surfaced, especially in Eastern Africa, and the foreign-expert component has been extensively scaled down during implementation and often replaced by local experts and bilateral sources. Such expertise was used and was less effective than anticipated for lack of good counterparts, poor timing or scheduling of the experts, neglect of the training role, or the preoccupation with tasks other than institutional development.

Conclusion

As the Economic Community of West African States (ECOWAS) moves toward the twenty-first century, it should now thoroughly set up new guidelines on how it can best achieve its goal. Over the years, ECOWAS has not lived up to its intended purpose for economic interdependence by member states; since there has been no effective implementation of common economic policies, it can achieve its goal through the help of the following recommendations. They are as follows: (a) that the Economic Community of West African States be headed by a career businessperson instead of one of the regional heads of state, (b) that a trans-West African highway be built to enable the free flow of goods to member countries, and (c) that there be no restriction for members of one state to travel to another.

However, the establishment of the Economic Community of West African States for Economic Interdependence must confine itself to the economic sphere since this is where progress appears likely. It should serve as a common market as a basis for an economic union; ECOWAS, under the leadership of a career businessperson, must be given wide powers to formulate, shape, and implement a community policy.

With an eye to the future and the ultimate aims of West African Economic integration, by the creation of more treaties, it is believed that in the minds of the founding fathers, the fusion of economic interests that began with the establishment of the community would generate or, at least, foster conditions favorable to more far-reaching political integration.

As stated in one of the recommendations, goods must be allowed to circulate freely within the Economic Community. For it to become a reality, persons must be allowed free movement. For it to have permanence, free currency exchange and fixed parities must be maintained with the union.

The true purpose of the ECOWAS must be to define new objectives, giving a fresh stimulus to West African interdependence. Initiatives on economic and monetary union, social-policy measures, and issues relating to enlargement must be explored.

Since the Economic Community of West African States is the engine of Western African Policy, the guardian of any treaty and the advocate of the region interests, members should be appointed by mutual agreement between the governments for a specified term. They should be required to act in complete independence for the good of the region.

Finally, criteria must exist to enable ECOWAS members to determine whether vital interests of one or more of its members really are at stake.

Bibliography

ECONOMIC COMMUNITY OF WEST AFRICAN STATES

Imposing Peace. (Liberia) (International). *The Economist* August 18, 1990. p. 37(2).
Cauldron of Emotions in West Africa. (Liberia's Civil War and West African Intervention) by Holman Jenkins Jr. il. vG. *Insight*. Dec. 10, 1990. p. 30 (2).

WEST AFRICA RICE DEVELOPMENT ASSOCIATION

Second Chance for Rice Research Center. (West Africa Rice Development Association) by John Walsh. il. v239 *Science*. Feb. 26, 1988. p. 969(2).

ECONOMIC POLICY
Africa

Politics: Key to Africa's Future (column) by Milton Allimadi. v384 *Journal of Commerce and Commercial*. Aril 20, 1990. p. 8A(1).

EUROPEAN COMMUNITY
Agricultural Policy

EC's New Farm Plan Seen No Help to GATT. (European Community General Agreement on Tariffs and Trade) by John Maggs. v387 *Journal of Commerce and Commercial*. Jan. 17, 1991. p. 10A(1).

EUROPEAN COMMUNITY
Finance

A Hard Road to Monetary Union. (European Community) by Graham Hallett. il. *Management Today*. September '90. p. 30(1).

EUROPEAN COMMUNITY
Finance

European Muddles toward a Freer Market. (European Community Works out Its Policies), column by David Brook. 33 col. in. *The Wall Street Journal*. Dec. 14, '90. p. A18(E), col. 4.

ECONOMIC INTEGRATION

Europe 1992. (Economic integration) by Gita Ghatt. v26. Finance and Development. June '89. p. 40(3) R5R1584. Automakers, Airlines, and Agriculture by Shawn Tully 58A2344.

International Labour Migration within a Common Market: Some Aspects of the EC experience. (European Common Market Studies). Sept. '88. p. 45(18) Holdings: This Puts Them on a Collision Course with the European Community's Goal of Creating an International Market after 1992. (Business). il. v317. *The Economist*. Nov. 17, '90. p. 83(2).

LANGUAGES

The Language of Europe. (Official Languages of Europe). (Europe) il. v314. *The Economist*. Jan. 20, '90. p. 54(1).

Executive Policy

MILITARY POLICY

Regional Defense Plan Urged for Europe. (European Community Proposed Security Policy). (International pages) by Alan Riding. 13, col. in v140, *The New York Times*. Dec. 8 '90. p. 3(L) col. 4.

International Labour Organization. 1992. *Analysis of Activities and Future Prospects*. Geneva.

International Labour Organization. 1992 *CIADFOR*.

Journal of European Industrial Training. 1993.

National Productivity Center (NPC). 1993.

Psacharopoulos, G. 1984. *Assessing Training Priorities in Developing Countries; Current Practice and Possible Alternative*. World Bank, Washington.

UNESCO/World Bank, 1992. *Joint Study of Technical Assistance in Bank-Financed Management Projects.*

World Bank/UNESCO. 1992. *Joint Study of Technical Assistance in Bank-Financed Education Projects.*

Index

A

ACP (African, Caribbean, and Pacific), 31
action-oriented courses, 47–48
African institutional strength, 10
agricultural policy, common, 35–37

C

Cameroon, 46–48, 50
CCT (common customs tariff), 26–27, 35
CEAO (West African Economic Community), 1, 60
CIADFOR (Inter-African Center for the Development of Vocational Training), 1, 51, 57, 62, 66, 79
civil service establishment, 12
collaboration, 14, 47, 59–60
community budget, 24, 32–33, 35, 37
community law, 28, 42
community market, 31, 37
community partners, 25
community policies, 35, 41, 75
consumer protection, 28, 32, 34
contracts, public, 42
cooperation, 20, 25, 31, 40, 53, 61–62, 65
  agreements, 31
  technological, 40–42
coordination, 19, 22–23, 43, 49, 52–54, 64
cost-reduction efforts, 6
Council of Europe, 21
Council of Ministers, 27–28
countries
  industrialized, 55, 62
  low-duty, 27
  low-income, 57
  member, 15, 31, 60, 75
  middle-income, 57
  poorest, 31, 43
Court of Justice, 28, 38–39
currencies, 23–24, 31–32
customs barriers, 26–27
customs duties, 26, 37
customs tariffs, common, 26–27, 35

D

deficiencies, 10, 12, 16, 52, 71–72
developing countries, 8, 31, 57, 59–60, 62–63, 66, 69, 79
development administration, 47–48

development projects, 11
  institutional, 64–65
  sectoral, 51

E

Eastern Africa, 71, 73
Economic Community of West African States for Economic Interdependence, 75
ECOWAS (Economic Community of West African States), vii, 5, 32, 75–77
educational innovation, 69
educational planning, 4, 6, 8, 12, 16, 68–69, 73
educational planning capacity, 9
educational research, 4, 6, 69
education management, 3, 9, 15, 67
education projects, 8
education systems, 69, 71
EEC, 26–27
EEC Treaty, 26, 33–34, 36
EMS (European Monetary System), 23
ESAMI (Eastern and Southern African Management Institute), 45, 62
European common market, 31–32
European Community, 20, 24–25, 32, 77–78
European Community's Council, 24
European Defense Community, 39
European Political Community, 39
European States, 20–21, 41
European Union, 20, 39

F

fieldwork, 59, 61
financial crises, 5–6, 68

financial management, 6–7, 12, 15, 47, 60, 72
free movement of goods, 5, 25, 27, 29

I

IBE (International Bureau of Education), 70
IIEP (International Institute for Educational Planning), 1, 68
ILO (International Labour Organization), 7, 15–16, 44, 51–52, 59–66
ILO Management Development Programme, 60
Institute of Public Administration and Management, 46, 48
institutional development, 4–9, 11, 15–17, 53, 57, 59, 67–73
  assistance, 71
  components, 9, 11, 71–72
  efforts, 10
  financing, 8
  objectives, 70
  project design, 70
institutional framework, 7, 19, 44, 60
institutional measures, individual, 19
institutional objectives, 16
institutional problem, fundamental, 10
institutional system, 11
institutional weaknesses, 7, 10
institution building, 17, 43, 59, 63, 67
  comprehensive, 65
  efforts, 10, 43
institutions
  management-development, 44, 60
  management-training, 44
  public-administration, 47–48

INTERFORE (Inter-American Vocational Training Research and Documentation Centre), 62
International Institute for Educational Planning, 8, 16, 68
intracommunity trade, 27

L

labor market, 49, 51–52, 58
Lome Conventions, 31

M

management
  approach, 47–48
  educational, 6, 8, 71, 73
  institutionalized, 11
  operations, vii
  quality of, 18, 47
  realities of, 47–48
  resource, vii, 3
  support, 65
  training, 8, 60, 72–73
  of vocational training, 14, 49, 62
management development, vii, 3, 7, 13, 16–19, 44, 59, 61
  institutions, 8, 14
  policies, 18, 44, 46
management institutions
  government-sponsored, 44
  self-sustained, 64

N

NEIDA (Network for Educational Innovation and Development in Africa), 8, 69
nonformal training, 49–50, 57
nonformal vocational-training system, 54–55

NPC (National Productivity Center), 1, 51, 79

O

O and M (organization and methods), 1, 12

P

performance improvement, 61
programs
  management-development, 18
  management-training, 44
  national management-development, 61
  sectoral, 61
  sector-development, 15
project
  design, 70–72
  development, 65
  documents, 67
  evaluation, 9
  identification, 70
  implementation, 9, 71–72
  management, 8, 61, 71–72
  phase, 64
public administration, 6, 13, 15, 44–46, 48

R

resources, 11, 16, 27, 32–33, 37, 46, 53
restrictions, 27–28, 75
  quantitative, 27, 31

S

school system, 16, 49, 52, 62
Second Education Project, 49
staff training, 13, 44, 46

Sub-Sahara Africa, vii, 3, 5, 7, 9–11, 13, 15–19, 21, 23, 25, 27, 29, 31, 33, 35, 37, 39, 41, 43, 45, 47, 49–51, 53–57, 61, 63, 65, 67, 69–73, 79

T

Technical Committee, 66
training institutions, 7, 13, 44, 49, 52, 54, 58, 65

U

UNDP (United Nations Development Programme), 1, 68–70
UNDP interregional project, 61
UNESCO (United Nations Educational Scientific and Cultural Organization), 1, 7–9, 15–16, 67–70, 79

V

vocational training, 1, 14, 17–18, 29, 33, 49–52, 56–58, 62–66
    institutions, 63, 66–67
    management of, 8–9, 16, 65, 72–73
    managing nonformal, 50–51, 53
    nonformal, 49, 55

W

World Bank (or the Bank), 8, 15, 61, 69–73, 79

www.ingramcontent.com/pod-product-compliance
Lightning Source LLC
Chambersburg PA
CBHW021545200526
45163CB00015B/1786